BLACK BELT
B·O·O·K·S

21ST CENTURY WARRIORS

Fighting Secrets of Mixed-Martial Arts Champions

Jason William McNeil

Photos by Rick Hustead

BLACK BELT B·O·O·K·S

21ST CENTURY WARRIORS

Fighting Secrets of Mixed-Martial Arts Champions

Jason William McNeil

Edited by Sarah Dzida, Raymond Horwitz,
Jeannine Santiago and Jon Sattler

Graphic Design by John Bodine

Cover Photography by Fernando Escovar

Back Cover Photography by Rick Hustead

Library of Congress Control Number: 2009906947
ISBN-10: 0-89750-177-2
ISBN-13: 978-0-89750-177-4

First Printing 2009

BLACK BELT BOOKS
A Division of **OHARA PUBLICATIONS, INC.**
World Leader in Martial Arts Publications

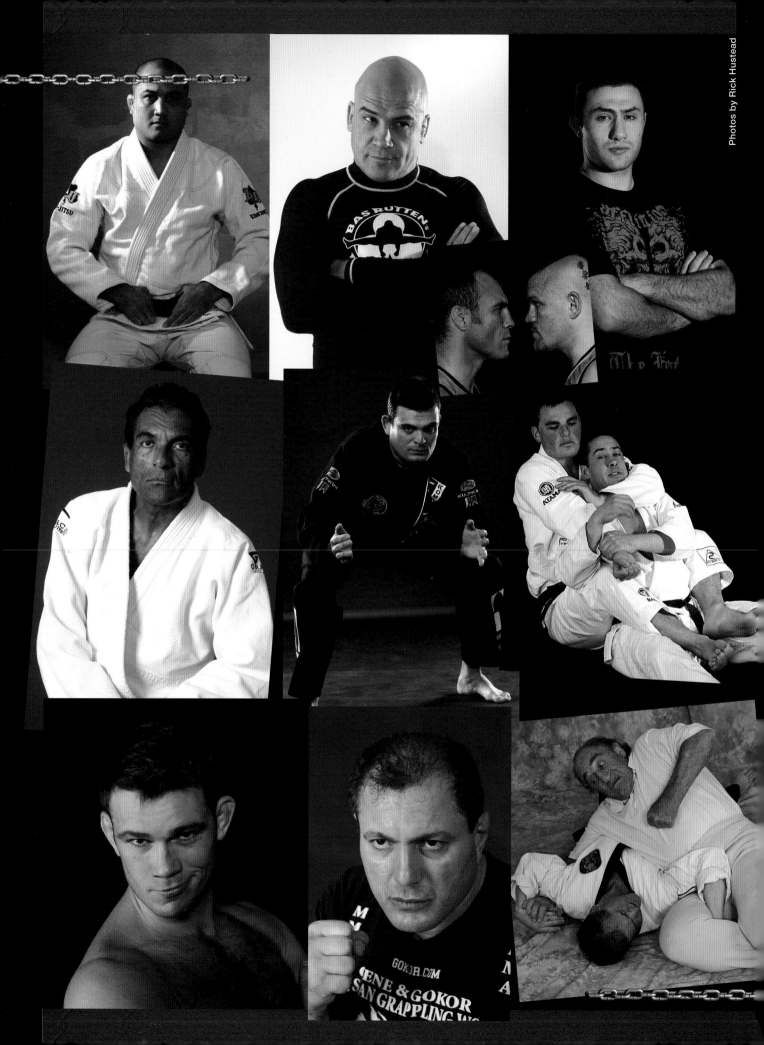

DEDICATION

This book is dedicated to the memory of Helio Gracie (1913-2009), who lit a candle to show the world it was in darkness.

—Jason William McNeil
2009

ACKNOWLEDGMENTS

Special thanks to Dr. Jerry Beasley, to *sensei* Ric "Papa San-Do" Anderton and to Rikki Rockett, the king of kick drums, hair spray and head locks. Thanks for opening the doors and making the introductions, gents!

—Jason William McNeil
2009

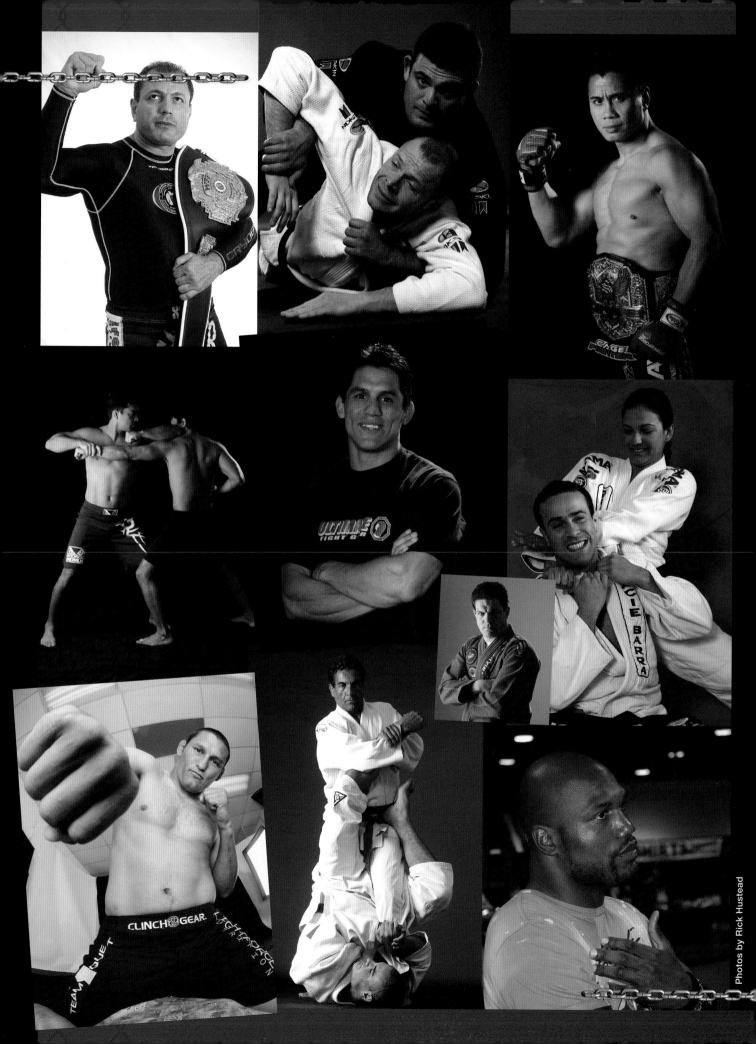

Photos by Rick Hustead

FOREWORD

In 1971, Black Belt Books, then known as Ohara Publications, released a book titled *20th Century Warriors: Prominent Men in the Oriental Fighting Arts*. A collection of profiles taken from the pages of *Black Belt* and *Karate/Kung Fu Illustrated* magazines, it was meant to be a veritable who's who of martial arts movers and shakers like Jigoro Kano, Gichin Funakoshi and Morihei Uyeshiba.

Obviously, the martial arts landscape has changed in the years since. Prominent men of the classical fighting arts have been replaced by mixed martial artists who dominate the scene. Kano and judo have stepped aside for the Gracies and Brazilian *jiu-jitsu*. Funakoshi's karate has taken a backseat to MMA superstars like Chuck Liddell.

The faces that represent the best and brightest have changed, which meant it was time to revisit and revise that 1971 title.

21st Century Warriors: Fighting Secrets of Mixed Martial Arts Champions profiles some of the fighters who define and represent the martial artist in the modern era. Like the history of martial arts, these fighters have had their triumphs and defeats. But no matter what they do or how they evolve, they remain relevant and unique examples of MMA champions. This book tells their stories.

—Editors of *Black Belt*
2009

TABLE OF CONTENTS

TABLE OF CONTENTS

INTRODUCTION

During the 20th century, as the Eastern martial arts were introduced to the Western world, the emphasis was always on "old" concepts. Even as these "new to us" fighting styles worked their way into the collective consciousness, entertainment media and commerce outlets across America, one could hear it in the language: Old was good.

"Venerable" masters, "ancient" arts, "33rd-generation" this and "34th-generation" that. "Unchanged from the time of the samurai" was a popular one, as was "secret wisdom of the ancients." It would be difficult to count how many "original fighting styles of the Shaolin Temple" popped into existence in the 1970s while David Carradine's *Kung Fu* "Grasshopper" on television conveniently provided a one-hour prime-time advertisement on a weekly basis. (Never mind the fact that many of those arts barely resembled any known style of kung fu, much less Shaolin—and some even wore karate uniforms and used Japanese terminology.)

Nevertheless, the message was clear: Old was good. The ancestors knew better than you do, so don't go messing around with martial arts that have remained unchanged for thousands of years (or, as we later found out in the cases of judo, karate, *aikido*, *taekwondo*, *wushu* and many others, at least since the mid-1950s). You don't go mucking around with tradition, boys and girls. And you *certainly* don't train in more than one style. Why that's tantamount to treason!

Then, as the war-torn 20th century shuddered, staggered and prepared to gasp its last breath, something phenomenal happened: Martial artists dropped all that baggage and started mixing it up, moving freely from school to school and system to system, picking and choosing from the buffet of knowledge and training available to the modern martial arts student and used whatever worked.

They also tossed aside whatever didn't.

As the 21st century dawned, a new sport led the way in the mixed-martial arts revolution. Following in the footsteps of the Ultimate Fighting Championship on mats, in cages and on TV screens

around the world, fighters punched, kicked, grappled and threw. They locked, choked and hit with their elbows and knees.

Suddenly, boxing looked kind of boring.

Like a cowboy boomtown, the early "gold rush" of UFC imitators enjoyed a certain wild and wooly element of lawlessness. When the dust finally settled, the new fightsport remained. The sports world—and that certainly of the martial arts—had changed forever.

Just like in those Wild West boomtowns, a certain breed of warrior has been drawn to the excitement, the blood lust—yes, even to the danger offered by living on the edge of the new frontier. Like the "quick-draw artists" and gunslingers of days passed, these fighting men (and women) have flocked—by hook or, occasionally, by crook—to wherever the action has been, eager to prove their worth, show their skills and, in the cases of a lucky few, rise to the top of a new, exciting and expanding field of combative competition.

These are the new heroes. These are the new fightin' pioneers. The MMA champions of today are the trailblazers for the fighters, the martial artists and the pugilistic sportsmen of tomorrow. They're the next generation's "venerable grandmasters," moving among us and competing today.

So what sort of person climbs into a cage with nothing but his skills, fists and a pair of 4-ounce gloves for protection? What sort of person has the guts, the drive and sheer force of will to ascend to the championship realm of a new fighting sport?

They're warriors, every one—pure and simple. They're unique. They're aggressive. Some are beautiful and charming, and some are well … ugly and occasionally obnoxious.

But each fighter profiled in this book represents some aspect of the warrior spirit of MMA competition at the dawn of the 21st century.

They are the *21st Century Warriors*.

—Jason William McNeil
2009

VITOR BELFORT

The Phenom Is Back

The life and times of Brazil's most popular MMA fighter: Vitor Belfort.

by Marcelo Alonso, photos by Pony Horton
FightSport October/November 2003

Vitor Belfort, a *jiu-jitsu* black belt under Carlson Gracie, has written his name in the history of mixed martial arts as one of the most explosive strikers ever to compete in the Ultimate Fighting Champion-

ship. At 19, the Brazilian showed the fighting world the importance of cross-training, and his youthful combination of world-class skills, athleticism and good looks got him dubbed "The Phenom."

However, a mix of sudden fame combined with three serious injuries has pinballed Belfort's career all over the map. Bad moments (losses to Randy Couture and Kazushi Sakuraba) were as common as amazing ones (the knockout of future PRIDE middleweight champion Wanderlei Silva and his recent performance at the UFC 43), making Belfort an enigma among the world's best fighters.

Yet when "The Phenom" fights, fans are only satiated by the spectacular knockouts that made him so feared when he began fighting in 1996. With his head screwed on straight again and various injuries behind him, Belfort, now 26, appeared to enter the ring at the UFC 43 in June 2003 a new man.

The importance of Belfort knocking out Marvin Eastman at the UFC 43 was obvious when his emotions got the best of him afterward. "I stopped [for] six months due to a very serious knee surgery and people always asked me about the old Belfort of the fast hands," the Brazilian said, fighting back the tears. "I'm very happy that I could bring the old Vitor back. This is the first time for a long time that I feel myself 100 percent. I wanted to fly in that octagon. I wanted to do everything at the same time—knees, hands, ground—but I couldn't show everything."

Under the Gracie Umbrella

Belfort displayed his potential in the 1994 Brazilian National Jiu-Jitsu Tournament. While everybody expected to see the black-belt category dominated by the likes of Royler and Renzo Gracie, Fabio Gurgel and Murilo Bustamante, the 17-year-old, 175-pound Carlson Gracie blue belt easily defeated each of his six opponents. "Vitinho," as he was nicknamed, submitted four of the six while winning both the heavyweight and open divisions.

Moving with Gracie to the United States, Belfort constantly trained in jiu-jitsu and *vale tudo* while working on his boxing in a Los Angeles gym. It was then that Gracie realized Belfort, 30 pounds heavier than when he excelled in the 1994 jiu-jitsu

tournament, was a phenom in the making.

"He is ready to beat anyone," the master revealed in May 1996. "He can beat Shamrock, Ruas. Great names of the UFC already came to my academy and proved his efficiency." At that time, Gracie even made a marketing plan to launch his young fighter. "He is like a son to me, and the Gracie name is really strong in the U.S., so he will be called Vitor Belfort Gracie," he said.

In Hawaii five months later, Belfort proved that he didn't need the Gracie name to be respected in the MMA world, needing mere seconds to knock out John Hess at SuperBrawl 2. In February 1997, he made his debut in the octagon at the UFC 12. Using his sharp, fast hands, Belfort stopped Tra Telligman in one minute 18 seconds and Scott Ferrozzo in just 52 seconds. Three months later, Belfort continued his amazing string by knocking out David "Tank" Abbott in only 53 seconds at the UFC 13.

The Kid Takes a Tumble

Being "The Phenom" was no bed of roses for the kid from Rio de Janeiro. In addition to reducing his time in the gym, Belfort used steroids to gain weight. From May 1997 (when he fought Abbott) to October 1997 (when he fought Randy Couture at the UFC 15), a lot of things changed. Tipping the scales at almost 230 pounds—far from his best physical condition—Belfort had lost his speed and was an easy target for Couture, who pounded him badly and forced a stoppage just after the eight-minute mark.

The loss—Belfort's first—was a nightmare in the new star's career. He quarreled with his master and soon Gracie stopped training him. Belfort bounced back, returned to his normal weight and submitted Joe Charles by armbar two months later at Ultimate Japan 1.

Belfort and Gracie came to an agreement nearly a year into their separation. A few months before Ultimate Brazil in October 1998, Belfort began training with his old mentor again. The result was one of the most impressive wins of his career: He knocked out Silva in his home country.

Just when things seemed to be good again, Belfort committed yet another mistake and paid an expensive price. Only two weeks after undergoing minor knee surgery, Belfort took $40,000 to step in the ring against Sakuraba at PRIDE 5 in April 1999. Once again, his fans were disappointed because Belfort lost badly to the Japanese star.

After dominating the first few minutes of the fight, Belfort broke his left hand while connecting with Sakuraba's head. From that point on, he had no chance and was punished for almost 16 minutes. "I didn't fight; I survived," said Belfort, who after the loss broke up with Gracie for good and started to train with the Brazilian Top Team.

Surgeries to the broken hand forced him out of the ring for almost a year. When he returned, Belfort employed a completely different game, one based on a ground-and-pound approach. Training extensively with American wrestler Darrell Gholar and BTT and lacking high-quality boxing sparring partners in Brazil, Belfort proceeded to bore his fans with plodding judges' decisions over Gilbert Yvel and Daijiro Matsui.

In 2001, Belfort accepted the challenge of facing American heavyweight Heath Herring when nobody wanted to face him. (He had just beaten Mark Kerr and Tom Erikson.) With a 40-pound weight disadvantage, Belfort walked away with a controversial decision victory. More important, fans were once again displeased. They wanted the old Belfort, the one who delivered amazing knockouts. Following the Herring bout, Belfort left BTT with Ricardo Arona, Allan Goes and Carlos Barreto and started training alone.

Toward the beginning of last year, Belfort finally had his chance to return to the UFC and challenge for the light-heavyweight belt against champion Tito Ortiz. "Vitor is in amazing shape. I just can't see how Ortiz could beat him," guaranteed Gholar after three months of training with Belfort leading up to the bout.

"I'm training a lot [in] *muay Thai* and wrestling. I feel in the best shape of my life," Belfort said at the time.

Once again, luck was not on Belfort's side. Two weeks before the fight, he suffered the second serious injury of his career: a large gash that cut muscles and ligaments in Belfort's left elbow after he slammed his arm through a glass window while training.

After four months of recovery, Belfort was back in great shape and preparing for the rescheduled Ortiz bout. However, this time Ortiz tore ligaments in his right knee and needed to have surgery. With Ortiz hurt, the UFC proposed a fight with Chuck Liddell—an offer that Belfort declined. He wanted the belt but had recently received an offer to take part in the Brazilian reality-TV show, *Casa dos Artistas*. While on the show, Belfort exposed mixed martial arts to the entire country.

Belfort left the reality show in May 2002 and was offered another shot to fight Liddell that June. Thanks to Belfort's newfound fame, the producer of the reality show, SBT, decided to broadcast the fight live on free television—something that had never happened in Brazil. Despite losing to Liddell by decision, Belfort brought in a record rating for the 11 p.m. time slot.

Distraction or Attraction?

The Brazilian media first noticed Belfort in 1997 when he began dating Marinara Costa, a famous model featured in one of the best-selling editions of *Playboy* magazine. Belfort was invited on many TV shows, which is a rarity for fighters.

Good looks and a friendly smile opened many doors for Belfort. In 2001 he found himself with another model, Joana Prado—the most desired woman in Brazil. Her *Playboy* appearance set a record in Brazil with 1.2 million copies sold. When she publicly presented Belfort as her boyfriend, the fighter's status skyrocketed throughout the country. By the start of 2002, he was invited to play himself (a vale tudo champion) in *O Clone*, the highest-rated Brazilian soap opera on Rede Globo, the largest TV network in Brazil.

Criticized by many fighters for his TV appearances, Belfort is slowly changing the view that Brazilian mainstream media has about fighters.

Today, thanks to him, more programs and newspapers are giving time and space to mixed martial arts. Because of that, many people know Antonio Rodrigo "Minotauro" Nogueira and Silva.

No other fighter in Brazil has ever garnered anything close to Belfort's popularity. Walking the streets of São Paulo with Belfort and fiancee Prado is like walking with Hollywood stars. "Our TV just gives space to soccer," he says. "Brazilian people want to have their Rocky Balboa." And Vitor Belfort is the right man for the job.

GINA CARANO

Black Belt's Full-Contact Fighter of the Year 2007: Gina Carano

by Tom Callos, photo by Edward Pollard
Black Belt December 2007

In less than four years, Gina Carano has become one of the most recognizable women on the American fight scene. A talented martial artist and a surefire crowd-pleaser, she's demonstrated her skills in kickboxing and mixed martial arts time and again. Considering her genetics, her rise to

CARANO ON THE SCREEN

MOVIES

Blood and Bone
(2009) "Veretta" (stars Michael Jai White, co-starring Julian Sands and Michelle Lee)

Ring Girls
(2005) Herself

GAMES

Command & Conquer: Red Alert 3
(2008) "Natasha Volkova"

VIDEOS

American Gladiators Ultimate Workout
(2008) Herself (as "Crush")

Fatal Femmes Fighting: Asian Invasion
(2008) Herself

TELEVISION

EliteXC Saturday Night Fights
(Series—2008) Herself
Episodes 1.1 and 1.3

The Late Late Show With Craig Ferguson
(Episode dated September 29, 2008) Herself

American Gladiators
(Series—2008) "Crush"
16 Episodes

E:60
(Series—Episode dated May 13, 2008) Herself

Inside MMA
(Series—Episode 2.7) Herself

ShoXC: Elite Challenger Series
(Series—Episode 1.1) Herself

EliteXC
(Series—2007) Herself

Destiny
(2007) Herself

Countdown to Destiny
(TV Documentary—2007) Herself

—Compiled by Jason William McNeil

the top isn't surprising.

Carano comes from a family of remarkable athletes. Her father, Glenn Carano, was a University of Nevada, Las Vegas, star quarterback. In the 1970s, he played for the Dallas Cowboys as backup quarterback behind the legendary Roger Staubach. Tall and lean, he shares with his daughter a face and physique that could have come from a Renaissance sculpture. Carano's uncles are also athletic, each more than 6 feet tall, the kind of men you wouldn't want to meet in a dark alley.

But Gina Carano doesn't need her uncles for protection; she can take care of herself. The 24-year old Nevadan has made herself one of the best-known female faces in the predominantly male sport of mixed martial arts, where she's garnered a 4-0 record. And she's built a 12-1-1 record in *muay Thai* kickboxing. Even though she's participated in the fight sports for a relatively short time, she's inspired a new generation of female athletes to regard full-contact competition as something women can do rather than just watch.

Carano's celebrity has stemmed in part from her appearances on historic televised fight cards and from coverage she's received on high-profile TV shows. Her first MMA bout pitted her against Leiticia Pestova in the first women's MMA match sanctioned by the Nevada State Boxing Commission. In February 2007, Carano showed up on Showtime in what was billed as the fight of the night—and she soundly defeated her foe, Julie Kedzie. It was the first time a women's MMA event was televised on a premier cable network.

Carano was also featured in the MSNBC documentary *Warrior Nation* and the independent film *Ring Girls.* The latter served as a catalyst for her role as a coach and mentor in *Fight Girls,* an Oxygen-channel reality series that followed a squad of female kickboxers as they competed against each other to earn a spot on a fight card in Thailand.

For those accomplishments and more, Gina Carano has been inducted into the *Black Belt* Hall of Fame as 2007 Full-Contact Fighter of the Year. When asked how she feels to have joined the

CARANO IN THE CAGE

EVENT	DEFEATED	METHOD
EliteXC: Heat (October 4, 2008)	**Kelly Kobold**	**Decision** (Unanimous)
EliteXC: Primetime (May 31, 2008)	**Kaitlin Young**	**TKO** (Doctor Stoppage)
EliteXC: Uprising (September 15, 2007)	**Tonya Evinger**	**Submission** (Rear-Naked Choke)
EliteXC: Destiny (February 10, 2007)	**Julie Kedzie**	**Decision** (Unanimous)
Strikeforce: Triple Threat (December 08, 2006)	**Elaina Maxwell**	**Decision** (Unanimous)
WPFC 1: World Pro Fighting Championships (September 15, 2006)	**Rosi Sexton**	**KO**
World Extreme Fighting (June 10, 2006)	**Leticia Pestova**	**KO**

—Compiled by Jason William McNei

RANO IN THE POLLS!

End 2008—Ranked No. 5 of
Top 10 Most Influential Women
erica" by Yahoo.com

2008—"Gina Carano"
d "Fastest-Rising Search"
ogle.com

008—Named "Third Most
ed Person" on Yahoo.com

ompiled by Jason William McNeil

ranks of legends like Don Wilson, Jean-Yves Theriault Kathy Long, Randy Couture, Ken and Frank Shamrock Tito Ortiz and Chuck Liddell, she had the following to say

"I feel very honored and humbled about being included in the *Black Belt* Hall of Fame. Two of the greatest compliments this has given me is that readers voted for me and that I'll be added to a Hall of Fame [filled with] names respect and look up to. Thank you all for watching me and staying with me throughout my career. My goal in life is to follow what God's plan is for me and allow him to shine his light through me. I cannot say where I will be in five years—scratch that, tomorrow—but I know tha wherever you find me, I will remain true to myself with a genuine smile on my face and happiness in my heart God bless, listen to your heart and never stop fighting for what you believe."

GOKOR CHIVICHYAN

Profile: Gokor Chivichyan

by Jason William McNeil, photos by Rick Hustead
BOOK EXCLUSIVE

Carrying (and Passing) the Torch

A former Soviet powerhouse, a current American grappling guru, a perennial almost-Olympian and the winner of more matches in more countries than anyone can easily count, Armenian-born Gokor Chivichyan has traveled a long, hard and altogether unusual road in the pursuit of mixed-martial arts mastery.

It's a road, however, that has left him a unique figure in the MMA world: a champion and trainer of champions, possessed of an atypical mix of fighting styles (if such a creature as the "typical" no-holds-barred fighter exists) whose little *dojo* in Southern California, Hayastan MMA Academy, bears the metaphorical track marks out front of the MMA world beating a path to his door.

Sharing training space, students and heaping helpings of mutual admiration with no less a grappling godhead than his partner and mentor "Judo" Gene LeBell, Chivichyan has become the "go-to guy" for up-and-coming champions looking to learn at the feet (and hands, knees and elbows) of a teacher who came up the hard way, knows the ins and outs and ups and downs of the no-holds-barred fight game, and—perhaps most important—is possessed of a skill set altogether unique in a game in which competitors are always looking for a new hold, a new technique, a new *anything* to give them that elusive edge that puts them over the top and into the winner's circle.

However, as the oft-quoted maxim more or less goes, Chivichyan's thousand-mile journey to MMA mastery began with a single step—and that first step was taken behind what was then known as the Iron Curtain.

Winters of Discontent

In 1968, at the tender age of 5, young Chivichyan began what would become his world-spanning grappling odyssey at the unassuming

Dinamo Wrestling Studio in Yerevan, Armenia. A scant year later, he crossed over (already mixing his martial arts) to begin training in the skills of *sambo*, a hybrid martial art originally developed by the Soviet Union to train the military and various law-enforcement officials and later modified and codified into a less-deadly but no-less effective competitive sport version. (See Page 27 for more about sambo, a brutally elegant art that is just being discovered and explored by Western fighters and which will, no doubt, be enthusiastically absorbed into the ever-evolving mixed-martial arts matrix.)

Chivichyan recalls that even at that young age what would become his lifelong love of fighting had swallowed him whole. He "trained four to five hours a day" and made a point of matching with "larger and more advanced students, often besting them in class."

In 1971, with less than four years of training under his belt, Chivichyan competed in his first tournament, the Armenian Junior National Sambo Championship. Looking back more than 40 years, Chivichyan swells with a champion's pride as he

recalls that he "won all his matches quickly and with ease."

At his second Armenian Junior National Sambo Championship, 9-year-old Chivichyan decided to move up to a "more challenging" division and won first place in the 10- to 12-year-old division, taking the gold medal and qualifying to travel to Russia to compete in the 1972 Russian Junior National Sambo Championship.

For a man who has since gone on to win championships in numerous arenas on multiple continents, it might seem strange that he points to 1973 as a "pivotal year" in his life, but he maintains that it was the events of that year that set him firmly on the path he follows to this day. It was in 1973 that the evolving young Chivichyan began training in yet another grappling art, judo, promptly winning the Armenian National Judo Championships before moving on to the Russian National Judo Championships.

At the 1973 Russian games, Chivichyan experienced his first competitive loss. After making it to the finals, he lost by decision to a three-time Soviet national champion.

While coming home with a silver medal from a national championship would have been a high watermark for most competitors, it nearly devastated Chivichyan, a boy for whom nothing less than first place was remotely palatable.

He remembers that his first loss "haunted" him, driving him to train even harder. "I promised myself that I would never lose another competition in my life," Chivichyan says.

The first step in keeping that promise to himself was executed the following year, when the young Armenian returned to sweep the Russian National Judo Championships and the Russian National Sambo Championships, bringing home gold medals from both events.

Continuing his fevered drive for competition and victory, the growing, evolving and always ambitious Chivichyan began taking the first tentative steps into the world beyond the Iron Curtain. From 1974 through 1980, Chivichyan racked up victories at competitions in Europe and at the

GOKOR'S GRAPPLING GRAB BAG

Sambo Leg Locks for Fun and Competition

According to Gokor Chivichyan, a world-traveled MMA champion with a bigger bag of tricks to draw from than perhaps any fighter outside of Gene LeBell (and even Chivichyan makes a point of staying on LeBell's good side), the leg locks of *sambo* offer a world of winning opportunities not presented in many other wrestling-style arts. Any forward-thinking mixed martial artist would be remiss to not include them in his arsenal of techniques.

"I love sambo, *jujutsu*, judo and grappling," Chivichyan says. "Like judo, sambo is more stand-up than arts like Brazilian *jiu-jitsu*, but sambo has very good leg attacks. Sambo is one piece of the pie. You need everything."

—JWM

World Games, culminating with him qualifying for the Soviet Olympic judo team.

Unfortunately, what could have been a Michael Phelps-style career high point was not to be because relative newcomer Chivichyan was "passed over for an older, more experienced athlete who went on to win the gold." Though Chivichyan felt a certain national pride in his team and country's victory, he couldn't help but be "greatly disappointed by not being able to compete in the Olympics."

Sadly, it wouldn't be the last time the chance to grapple for Olympic gold would slip just shy of his formidable grip.

Coming in From the Cold

A year after having his Olympic dreams dashed, Chivichyan and his family immigrated to the United States, where the young fighter eventually gravitated into the orbit of the legendary "Godfather of Grappling," Gene LeBell.

Although he recalls that times were tough and that he struggled to learn English while working, training and trying to learn as much as he could about American culture, the teenage Chivichyan was ecstatic to be taken under the wing of such a knowledgeable and legendary teacher as LeBell. "Gene taught me techniques I had never encountered before," Chivichyan says, "and I quickly added these techniques to my training."

Always keeping his dream of Olympic gold in mind, Chivichyan competed, trained and experimented constantly with the singular goal of competing (and winning) on the U.S. judo team at the 1984 Los Angeles Olympics.

From 1982 to 1984, Chivichyan competed in judo tournaments and no-holds-barred matches, "sometimes for money and sometimes just for the experience and excitement." His competitive drive took him all over North America as well as Europe, Japan and Thailand, where he was exposed to numerous styles of fighting and a smorgasbord of new techniques, all of which the ambitious Olympic hopeful sucked up like a dry sponge dropped in a lake. It was during this period that Chivichyan began to earnestly train in the skills of Western boxing and *muay Thai* (often called Thai kickboxing) to ramp up his striking game and augment his already devastating grappling skills.

In 1984, the Olympic gold medal would, once again, prove to be the elusive mistress that the determined young Chivichyan just could not manage to win over.

Discovering that he wouldn't be able to secure his U.S. citizenship in time to compete for the U.S. Olympic judo team, Chivichyan spent months flying back and forth between America

and Russia, fighting jet lag and every opponent placed in his path to secure a second spot on the Soviet Olympic judo team. Though his Herculean efforts were as successful as he could have made them (he did earn a spot on the Soviet team), Chivichyan's five-ringed dreams were once again dashed when the Soviet Union announced its boycott of the American-hosted 1984 Olympics in what many international observers interpreted as retaliation for the Americans' boycott of the previous 1980 Moscow Olympic Games in protest of the Soviet invasion of Afghanistan.

Whether for the United States or for the Soviet Union, in Los Angeles or in Moscow, Chivichyan just wanted a chance at the ultimate prize in competitive judo: the Olympic gold medal. He wanted a chance to show everyone everywhere that Gokor Chivichyan was the best *judoka* in the world, but once again, forces outside his control conspired to keep the laurel wreath just out of his grasp.

Succinctly summing up a world of frustration and pain over a dream twice deferred, Chivichyan simply says he was "devastated."

With true championship spirit, however, Chivichyan used his setbacks as fuel for further victory, training and competing like a madman throughout the mid-to-late 1980s. One of his more memorable victories came in Spain at the 1987 Judo International World Cup, where the Armenian blasted through nine opponents to defeat a powerful Frenchman by *ippon* ("full point") three minutes into the third round of the finals.

It was during this period of competitive frenzy that the always-inquisitive Chivichyan was introduced to the techniques of Brazilian *jiu-jitsu*, accepting several invitations to train and trade techniques with a number of Brazilian competitors with whom he remains friends.

Frozen Out Again

Belying the cliché, the third time definitely wasn't the charm when it came to Chivichyan and his dreams of an Olympic gold medal. The U.S. Judo Federation helped Chivichyan acquire his U.S. citizenship in November 1987 with the goal of sending the Armenian powerhouse to bring home the gold for America at the 1988 Olympics, but his "late citizenship" didn't allow Chivichyan enough time to acquire the necessary competitive points to compete in the 1988 Olympic Games.

For one final time, and again through no fault of his own, Chivichyan was denied a shot at an Olympic gold medal. While Chivichyan gasped in frustration, his would-be competitors no doubt breathed a collective sigh of relief.

With a long and unbroken stream of victories behind him, Chivichyan began, for the first time, to think of a future beyond the next competition or even the next Olympics. He turned his attention to training the next generation of fighting champions. He opened the Hayastan MMA Academy in Hollywood, California, in 1991, drawing hundreds of students from around the world.

Many of Chivichyan's students have gone on to become competitors and even champions in their own right in the realms of competitive judo and, of course, mixed martial arts. When MMA exploded in the 1990s, Chivichyan was perfectly poised to be on the advancing edge, sending his students forth to become champions in the Ultimate Fighting Championship, Extreme Fighting, PRIDE and many other organizations.

While reveling in his newfound role as *sensei*, Chivichyan's competitive nature could never be fully submerged. He emerged from the cocoon of his training hall to win the 1994 U.S. Judo Nationals, and he came out of retirement again in 1997 to answer an invitation to fight a much-ballyhooed match against a Japanese no-holds-barred champion by the name of Maeda. Before an electrified Alabama crowd and pay-per-view audience worldwide, Chivichyan showed anyone and everyone that he still had the stuff when he armbarred the Japanese champ into submission only 51 seconds into the first round.

It was that same year that Chivichyan was inducted into *Black Belt's* Hall of Fame as the 1997 Judo Instructor of the Year.

Partnered with his mentor LeBell ("I keep trying to retire," LeBell insists, "but Gokor won't

GOKOR AT A GLANCE

→ **Ninth Dan, Judo**

→ **Sixth Dan, Sambo**

→ **Sixth Dan, Jujutsu**

→ **Two-Time USSR Junior Judo National Champion**

→ **Two-Time USSR Junior Sambo National Champion**

→ **1984 Olympic Judo Team Member**

→ **1988 Olympic Judo Team Member**

→ **1994 USA Senior National Judo Champion**

→ **Multiple European and World Championships (NHB - MMA)**

→ **Submission Grappler**

→ **Wrestler**

→ **Western and Thai Boxing**

→ **Undefeated MMA Professional Record**

—Compiled by JWM

let me!") under the banner "Gene LeBell and Gokor's Grappling World," Chivichyan continues to teach the next generation of champions personally and through books and DVDs. He teaches self-defense and restraint techniques to the Los Angeles Police Department (from which he has received numerous commendations) and, like most other Southern California martial artists, turns up in the occasional movie and TV show. He maintains affiliate schools in America, Europe and in his homeland of Armenia. "[My] dream is that Gene LeBell and Gokor's Grappling World branches out across the world and that our students become even more successful than we have been," Chivichyan says.

In the meantime, one is hard-pressed to ever catch Chivichyan very far from the mats. He's always grappling, always fighting, always training, training, training—either with his students, with LeBell or on his own, moving through the motions of a world-class fighter with the drive and determination that makes a man a champion.

From a man with nothing left to prove, one can't help but wonder what all the intensity is about. Has he got one more surprise up his sleeve? Can a man who many say has been the best in the world but was thrice stopped just short of the big finish line be content with passing the torch to the next generation of champions? Or will his competitive nature pull him out of retirement once more? Most folks would say that, for a man with nothing left to prove, still harboring such a competitive spirit might seem absurd. Of course, most folks aren't still smarting about that one time they lost when they were 10. …

What the future holds for Chivichyan, only time will tell.

SAMBO: THE SOVIET UNION'S PRE-EMPTIVE STRIKE AT MMA!

Still largely unknown in the West, practitioners of the Russian grappling art or *sambo* are immediately recognizable by their traditional uniform of a red or blue "sambo jacket" (not unlike a judo *gi* top), gym shorts and "sambo shoes."

The brainchild of two Russian hand-to-hand combat experts, sambo (*neé "Cambo"* and even sometimes in all-caps "SAMBO") was the result of a national push from the highest levels of the Soviet government to synthesize an effective "national" empty-handed combat art from the various regional fighting traditions of the newly minted Union of Soviet Socialist Republics.

Sambo is an acronym in Russian that means "self-defense without weapons." Strangely, it was developed in two separate camps, led by two men largely in competition with one another for the title of "Father of Russian Sambo." Financed by monetary grants from the Soviet government's Department of General Military Training, both men were assigned to create a new, superior, "state" hand-to-hand art, drawing the best techniques from both Russo-Slavic fighting traditions and foreign arts—most notably Japanese *jujutsu* and judo.

Early development of what would become sambo began when combat trainer Victor Spiridonov started experimenting with the integration of judo techniques into native Russian styles. Having observed Jigoro Kano's distillation of various Japanese jujutsu skills and traditions into his own new wrestling art of judo, Spiridonov—a Russo-Japanese War veteran whose background included a broad cross section of native Russian fighting styles—became inspired to pursue a similar quest, distilling the best techniques from all the fighting styles at his disposal, creating a sort of "Soviet super-style" of all-purpose empty-hand fighting.

Meanwhile, sambo's other founder was pursuing a similar goal. One of the first foreigners to earn a *nidan* (second-degree black belt) under judo's founder Kano, Vasili Oshchepkov was a teacher of karate and judo to the Red Army's elite forces at the Central Red Army House.

Rather than as a result of its rival founders putting their differences aside to create a single new art, what became modern sambo was actually birthed in the cross-training that occurred between soldiers studying in both camps, from both men, as well as from supplementary assistance

in the art's 10-year genesis from Ivan Vasilievich Vasiliev and Anatoly Kharlampiev, who studied and gathered techniques from fighting arts around the world. (Despite Spiridonov and Oshchepkov's best efforts and fiercest rivalry, it is Kharlampiev who was ultimately awarded reverence as the "Father of Sambo." Whether this was merely because of his political connections or the fact that he used those connections to bring about the USSR Committee of Sport's acceptance of sambo as the official national combat sport of the Soviet Union in 1938 is still a matter of debate.

The chief ingredients in the martial bouillabaisse that is sambo come from the native fighting traditions of Tuvan *khuresh*, Yakuts *khapsagai*, Chuvash *akatuy*, Georgian *chidaoba*, Moldavian *trinta*, Armenian *kokh*, and Uzbek *kurash*, among several others, as well the aforementioned Japanese jujutsu, judo and karate, and various European styles of boxing (traditional and *boxe Francaise/savate*) and combative and Olympic wrestling.

Today, five general classifications of sambo exist for exploration and experimentation by any martial artist looking to throw some devastating new tricks in his bag.

"Sport sambo" is stylistically similar to judo, focusing on throws, the ground game and submissions but allowing leg locks but prohibiting chokeholds in competition.

In contrast, "self-defense sambo" allows a wider range of brutal techniques, practiced against unarmed and armed attackers. Self-defense sambo is to sport sambo what judo is to jujutsu.

"Combat sambo" is practiced by the Russian military and includes weapons training. Of the five styles of sambo, combat sambo competitions most resemble modern MMA and no-holds-barred events, with lots of striking and grappling thrown into the mix.

"Special sambo" is a specialized arsenal of techniques and training based in combat sambo but developed to meet the specific skills and situations of Russian special forces and law-enforcement personnel.

"Freestyle sambo" is a 2004 creation of the American Sambo Association, designed to encourage judo and jujutsu players to compete in sambo events. Like sport sambo, the competition concentrates on throws, the ground game and submissions. Leg locks and chokes are also permitted, but striking techniques are prohibited.

RANDY COUTURE

Randy Couture

Hot off the heels of his victory over Tito Ortiz at the UFC 44, the new UFC light-heavyweight champion reveals the driving force behind his indomitable will to win.

by Josh Gross, photos by Rick Hustead
FightSport December 2003/January 2004

You sit down at ringside, anticipating a fight that had been discussed and dissected ad nauseam. You watch Randy Couture, 40 years young, stride confidently into the ring, absorbing the atmosphere of the charged arena. Similarly, you watch Tito Ortiz, 28, stomp his way toward his challenger—rushing, it seems, to get it over with. Over the course of five rounds, you watch in amazement as Couture, a man you've labeled the greatest mixed martial artist of the past decade, performs in a manner bordering on the supernatural.

After it's done, you sit back, shake your head in disbelief—and admiration—and ponder how anyone could have ever picked him to lose. Then

the cynic in you, the jaded journalist who can't take anything at face value, starts to doubt what your eyes just saw. You ask yourself questions you wouldn't articulate unless you were sure.

Another voice surfaces: the voice of your inner fan, the voice that put you in this privileged seat in the first place. It tells you to shut up and enjoy what you just witnessed. It says: Don't you realize guys like Randy are special? You may never see anyone like him again. You're ruining it. Stop being a critic for a second and remember how it feels to be a fan.

You listen and agree. The tough questions sink back into the shadows, lying in wait for those who deserve to face them.

Legacy

Randy "The Natural" Couture had already secured his place among the sport's greats. There was no need for him to drop from heavyweight to a 205-pound light-heavyweight and fight the ultra-hazardous Chuck Liddell at the UFC 43. Upon returning to the octagon following consecutive setbacks to Josh Barnett and Ricco Rodriguez (the latter leaving Couture with impaired vision after an elbow strike shattered an eye socket), even the 6-foot-1-inch fighter's staunchest supporters had every right to be concerned.

"I could have easily quit after the Josh Barnett or Ricco Rodriguez fights and been upset and depressed," Couture tells FightSport. "But that's never really been my nature."

Indeed. For a man whose competitive roots were planted while growing up in the suburbs of Seattle, where he lived with his single mother and two sisters, walking away from anything has never been his style.

Discussion of Couture's legacy has almost always focused on his in-ring accomplishments. Unlike some—like Ortiz, for example, who foolishly insinuated he wanted to be remembered alongside Muhammad Ali—Couture has repeatedly suggested that his standing as a fighter is best left "for other people to decide."

Couture's most important achievements

sprout from anything associated with family and fatherhood. At 18, with ambitions to compete as an Olympic wrestler percolating near the point of realization, life dealt Couture the starkest of wake-up calls.

"I found myself in a situation where I was having a kid," he says. His life and its pursuits barely out of the starting gates, Couture recognized the distinct possibility that dreams were destined to remain unfulfilled. "I thought that [it] was over," he admits.

As a child, Couture rarely interacted with his father, seeing him only on birthdays or Christmas. Even if it meant forgoing a chance at Olympic gold, he was hellbent on making sure his children would never feel like they missed out by not having a father in their lives. "I wasn't going to be like my father and not be there for my kid," Couture says.

Thanks to the foresight of his mother, Sharan Courounes, who "instilled a work ethic … a competitiveness that couldn't come from anywhere else," Couture says he handled the stressful situation the best way he knew how.

Two years later, Couture had fathered a baby sister, Aimee, for his toddler son, Ryan. Needing a way to support the growing family, he enlisted in the U.S. Army. Over the next six years, Couture was able to provide for two young children and a wife by serving his country. Surprisingly, his time in the Army also helped resurrect Olympic dreams that Couture was sure had been snuffed out.

Failure

If there was one thing Couture had always hoped to become it was an Olympian. From the moment he strapped on a pair of skis, he had ambitions of competing against the world's best in the downhill or slalom. Purse strings, however, were tight in the Couture household. Consequently, by fifth grade he spent his time wrestling rather than bunny-hopping down powdered slopes.

Upon graduating from Lynnwood High School in Lynnwood, Washington, in 1981, Couture

moved on to military life. It was during this time that he became a force among American Greco-Roman wrestlers, a discipline he picked up after enlisting. In 1988, the same year he became a World Military Games and U.S. Armed Forces champion, Couture earned the first of his three U.S. Olympic team alternate spots.

Alternate status, however, was not Couture's idea of a dream fulfilled. After discharging from the military, he enrolled at wrestling powerhouse Oklahoma State University in 1990. Once there, he earned All-American honors three times, twice becoming a National Collegiate Athletic Association runner-up while winning two national championships with the Oklahoma State Cowboys.

His many victories at the collegiate level, however, did little to placate his desire to land an Olympic invitation. In 1992, Couture's second failure to make the Olympics was compounded by a collapsing marriage. Soon after, he divorced his wife of 11 years.

Out of the military, single, a college graduate and with his children moving into adolescence, Couture began a new phase of life that saw him concentrate on earning a spot on the 1996 Olympic wrestling team that would compete in Atlanta. Despite being an odds-on favorite to make the squad, he fell short yet again. Clearly, his failure to make an Olympic team ranks as the biggest disappointment of his tenure as a competitive athlete.

"I was the guy who everyone expected to make the team, the No. 1 guy coming in," he remembers. "Certainly, when you don't come through and you don't wrestle to your best ability, you have to evaluate that."

Greatness

"There's no deep-seated internal thing that drives me to get out there and fight. It's not an emotional thing—for me it's just kind of who I am," Couture explains when asked what motivates him. Upon further review, there might be more to his insatiable desire to compete than he lets on.

While his mother may have provided an infrastructure for success, Couture's father could have unintentionally provided the impetus for the champion's ceaseless desire. He missed much of his son's childhood and was absent from his life during the decade after Couture married his first wife.

"Part of the drive I have on some level is [knowing] I'm going to make it. In a lot of ways, [I'm] bound and determined not to be like [my father] was, at least from my perspective," Couture explains.

Once that is understood, it's easier to make sense of Couture as a fighter. Stepping into the octagon as a novice in 1997, "The Natural" won his first four fights. This winning streak culminated in a decision victory over Maurice Smith at Ultimate Japan 1, which earned Couture the first of two Ultimate Fighting Championship heavyweight championships.

Six years and two title reigns later, he continues to step up and fight the best. When offered an opportunity to drop down in weight and fight Liddell (the No. 1 contender in the UFC's light-heavyweight division) at the UFC 43, Couture jumped at the chance.

Most pundits thought he was setting himself up for a third consecutive beating and a forced retirement. In reality, not only did he trounce Liddell, add another name to an impressive ledger of victims and earn the UFC light-heavyweight interim title, Couture insisted the victory was also a first step toward returning integrity to the weight division—a promise other fighters simply would not have made.

Next, of course, was the destruction of Ortiz at the UFC 44, which solidified Couture as the undisputed 205-pound UFC champion. More important, it confirmed his place in the annals of MMA history. Fifty years from now, his name will be uttered as one of the sport's greats.

It appears that today's top light-heavyweight fighters will have to risk facing the 40-year-old dynamo if they wish to be spoken of in the same light because, as he says, "I'm not going to set any limits on myself. I think I get better each time I step out there. As long as I'm physically able to

Randy Couture with Chuck Liddell
and Dana White.

train and compete at this level [and] prepare myself the way I think I should prepare for these fights, I'll continue to compete."

Couture has found a bastion of competition in the mixed martial arts that requires strength in mind, body and spirit. It demands everything we expect from a great man. In some ways, it also frees him to explore an artistic self-expression in the ring.

"I think we're all striving to be the best, and that's an opportunity to get out there and be the best," explains Couture, now remarried and father to another son, 5-month-old Caden. "That's the motivating factor for me. I want to get out there and show what I'm capable of. It's something that I love to do, which is not something a lot of people can say."

GRACIE LEGACY

by Jason William McNeil
BOOK EXCLUSIVE

Gracie Technique: The Guard

While professor Jigoro Kano was busily inculcating his new sport of judo (which he evolved from samurai fighting skills of *jujutsu*) into a worldwide competitive phenomenon, Japan's battlefield art was sowing seeds in faraway lands that wouldn't bear fruit for decades.

At the end of the 20th century, judo sat comfortably at the top of the heap, firmly established as the world's most successful martial sport. It had held the distinction of being the only martial art included as an Olympic sport. Jujutsu's lesser-known stepbrother (at that time) had been steadily growing, spreading and evolving. And soon, it would burst out of Brazil onto the international stage, changing the face of martial arts forever.

Without Brazilian *jiu-jitsu*, there would be no mixed martial arts as we know them today.

And without the Gracies—a fighting family dozens strong and generations deep— there would be no Brazilian jiu-jitsu. Period.

How, then, did the fighting arts of the samurai find their way to the sun-kissed shores of Brazil? And how did a single family usher in a martial arts revolution?

As with most sprawling, transcontinental tales, it's best to begin at the beginning.

Mitsuyo Maeda, The Count of Combat

Mitsuyo Maeda, also nicknamed Esai, was born in Aomori, a prefecture in Japan, (his date of birth is alternately given as 1878 and 1880) where he studied the traditional samurai unarmed fighting art of *tenshin shinyo jujutsu*. At age 18, Maeda moved to Tokyo to attend Tokyo Senmon School and began formal training at Kano's Kodokan in 1897. By all accounts, he was a talented and dedicated student who quickly rose through the *dojo*'s ranks to establish himself as one of the Kodokan's top young *judoka*.

In 1904, following up on growing American interest in judo (led by President Theodore Roosevelt, who was trained in the art under another legendary judoka Yoshitsugu Yamashita), Maeda was tapped to accompany his *kohai* (senior, i.e., "upperclassman") and instructor, Tsunejiro Tomita, on an exhibition and demonstration visit to the United States.

However, Tomita and Maeda's only joint demonstration at the U.S. Military Academy at West Point was deemed a failure. The judo ambassadors demonstrated *kata* in the Japanese fashion, but the purpose of the techniques was largely lost on the attendees. Challenged to prove the practicality of their fighting skills, Maeda matched with a collegiate wrestling champion. The American pinned Maeda and declared victory, but the Japanese practitioner was apparently unfamiliar with western wrestling rules and continued to fight. Eventually, he gained a particularly brutal joint lock on the student, who tapped out.

Incensed, the Americans insisted that Tomita, the instructor, accept a challenge match. The Kodokan *sensei*, unable to refuse without losing face, accepted the challenge and promptly lost when the much larger American simply rushed and tackled him, pinning Tomita's smaller Japanese frame under his heavy one.

After the debacle of the West Point demonstration, Tomita and Maeda parted company. Tomita traveled to the West Coast, while Maeda remained in New York. After winning several more challenge matches, Maeda secured a part-time job teaching at Princeton University. Maeda also made several attempts at teaching privately, but he found American students unresponsive to his harsh Japanese teaching methods. The situation quickly left him financially strapped.

To make quick cash, Maeda violated the Kodokan's strict code of ethics and began fighting for money—most notably against a professional wrestler from Brooklyn nicknamed "Butcherboy." The fight was billed as a "wrestling vs. judo" match, and it was Maeda's first step on his long journey through the world of professional fighting. Maeda won the match and became something of a celebrity among New York's Japanese population.

Deciding to take his fighting show on the road, Maeda traveled to Europe. In Spain, he acquired the professional name that would follow him the rest of his life: *"Conde Koma"* (Spanish for "Count of Combat").

During his travels, Maeda cultivated a habit that would later turn up in his pupils: generating notoriety by publicly challenging famous fighting champions. In England, Maeda called out a Russian wrestling champ who had been quoted in the newspapers as saying that wrestling was superior to judo. Surprisingly, the Russian declined Maeda's challenge, claiming that he had been misquoted. Also declining Maeda's challenge was American heavyweight boxing champion Jack Johnson, though certainly not for the same reasons.

Fighting his way around the globe, Maeda eventually traveled through Latin America, where he settled in Belém, Brazil, in 1915 (though he continued to fight in the United States, Mexico and Cuba). In addition to his trademark challenge matches, Maeda began teaching judo to São Paulo police force, army college cadets and a few hearty civilians. Among his judoka was a young man named Carlos Gracie.

Despite all his worldwide travels, reputed 2,000 challenge match victories and the prestige of instructing Brazil's professional peacekeepers and fighting forces, it was the then-teenaged Carlos who would most famously carry on the Count of Combat's fighting tradition, bearing the seed he planted in Brazil to fruition on a worldwide stage.

Despite several invitations from the Japanese government to return to his homeland—including an offer to pay the full cost of his return trip (in recognition of his status as a fighter and his altruistic efforts to assist Japanese immigrants in Brazil during a time of high anti-Japanese sentiment during the days leading up to World War II)—Maeda instead became a Brazilian citizen and remained in his adopted homeland, marrying twice and fathering two daughters. Supposedly, Maeda's second wife feared that if he went to Japan, he would never return to Brazil.

Despite his steadfast refusal of the Japanese government's offer of a return trip, Maeda's last words, spoken on his deathbed the following year, were reportedly said to be, "I want to drink Japanese water. I want to go back to Japan."

Conde Koma's Way

Showing his early schooling in old-school combative jujutsu—as well as a knack for brazen self-promotion that would pass undiluted to his martial descendents—Maeda maintained that judo was the ultimate form of self-defense, stating on numerous occasions that the Western arts like wrestling, boxing and fencing had become so sportified as to have lost most of their combative effectiveness. (The fact that Kano created judo to be a competitive sport by intentionally removing traditional jujutsu's most effective and dangerous fighting techniques didn't seem to factor into the Count of Combat's thinking).

Maeda's personal fighting strategies often revolved around leading with *atemi waza* (strikes)—elbows and low kicks—to set an opponent up for a throw. He would then follow with a finishing technique delivered on the ground, such as a joint lock or choke.

In his autobiography, Maeda said that he took the Kodokan judo he had been taught, focusing especially on the techniques of *taryu shiai* judo—judo skills taught and practiced specifically for matches against other schools—and refined it, through his experiments and experience fighting around the world, into the simplest, most effective methods of unarmed combat, particularly against what he perceived as the particular weaknesses of Western wrestling and boxing. It should also be noted that the judo Maeda had learned, as it was taught before World War II, included numerous locks and chokes that were later excluded from the Kodokan curriculum because they were illegal in sporting competition.

In Brazil, Maeda found a populace already culturally inclined toward wrestling, rather than trading punches, to settle disagreements. In much the same way that Japanese *karate-do* changed into *taekwondo* to better suit the Korean cultural preference for combative kicking, Japanese judo quickly found its way to the ground as the Maeda's students adapted jujutsu's brutal grappling elements to their own cultural characteristics.

Carlos Gracie: Start the Revolution

Carlos Gracie was the son of Gastão Gracie, a prominent Brazilian politician who aided Maeda in his efforts to assist Japanese immigrants. In gratitude for his father's help, Maeda agreed to teach 19-year-old Carlos his refined and combat-tested version of Japanese judo. Carlos proved an eager student, training with Maeda and several of his assistant instructors.

Despite his small stature, Carlos proved to be a adept fighter. His younger brothers—Oswaldo, Gastão, Jorge and Helio—soon followed suit. Through the lens of hindsight, it could be said that this was the moment of conception for the Gracie family's fighting dynasty. The brothers quickly made a name for themselves in demonstrations, street fights and—using their sensei's favorite promotional tactic—challenge matches throughout Brazil.

By 1925, the Gracie family's reputation as skilled, effective fighters was well-enough established that Carlos opened the first "Gracie Jiu-Jitsu Academy" that year in Belém.

Though he was well-known as a fighter himself—most notably against a "Japanese giant" known as Giomori, whom he fought twice to a pair of draws—Carlos turned his attention to running and building his school, leaving most of the challenging and fighting to his younger brothers. Of said siblings, Helio Gracie would prove the standout scrapper.

Establishing the Dynasty

From the age of 17, Helio was known as the family's fiercest fighter. Early victories over boxer Antonio Portugal (whom Helio defeated in 30 seconds) and a series of Japanese judoka over the ensuing years (including champions Namiki, Miyake and Kato) prompted a smarting Japanese judo contingent to finally summon the services of Masahiko Kimura (multiple winner of the All-Japan Judo Championship before and after the World War II) to put the scrappy Brazilian in his place.

In 1951, Helio faced off in a "judo rules" (no strikes, wearing *judogi* jackets) fight against the much larger Kimura in a gym next to Brazil's largest soccer stadium. The two battled for 15 grueling minutes, with Kimura generally controlling the match until Helio finally conceded defeat.

It was the first defeat in Helio's career, but anyone expecting an explosion of Latin temper would be sorely disappointed. Showing

exquisite grace in defeat and setting a shining example of true sportsmanship, Helio praised Kimura's skills—and continued to do so for the rest of his life. In fact, the armbar that finally forced Helio's submission was dubbed the *kimura* armbar and is taught by that name in Gracie Jiu-Jitsu Academy branches to this day.

Throughout his long and storied fighting career, Helio's only other defeat was at the hands of former student Valdemar Santana. According to Helio's son, Rorion, the accomplished Gracie academy fighter had had a falling out with Helio and denigrated him in a newspaper. The two agreed to settle their differences with a challenge match.

What followed was what may have been one of the longest and most brutal matches in jiu-jitsu history. On May 24, 1955, Helio fought the younger and larger Santana on national television at Rio de Janeiro's Central YMCA in a *vale tudo* rules contest. The match lasted a grueling three hours and 40 minutes, ending with a Santana victory via a kick to the kneeling Helio's head.

It would be Helio's last fight, but the Gracies were far from done with Valdemar Santana.

Carlos' son, Carlson Gracie, challenged Santana to a fight to avenge his family's honor. Carlson defeated Santana in the first of what would be six matches between the career rivals. Despite a half-dozen tries, Santana never managed to get the upper hand on the younger Gracie, losing outright to him four times and struggling to ties twice. For his efforts, Carlson earned the moniker "King Carlson."

Revolution Evolution!

According to the Gracie family, the art of Gracie jiu-jitsu further evolved under Helio's care. Lacking the size and strength of his brothers, Helio was forced to modify the art's techniques to rely less on muscle and more on skill and "maximizing leverage." Family tradition has it that Helio simply couldn't get out of

certain holds using the techniques his brother had taught him, so he had to either admit defeat or invent new ones. Not surprisingly, his inventions became the foundation of the art now known worldwide as Gracie jiu-jitsu.

To achieve escape velocity and make its way around the world, however, the Brazilian-based martial art would need more than just great fighters—although the prolific Gracie clan had provided those in abundance. It would need the ambition and vision of a marketing genius—a man who could bring the self-promoting spirit of the Count of Combat to the modern multimedia stage.

Little did the Gracie family know that such a man walked among them—and he was blood.

"The Baddest Man in the World" and the Birth of the Ultimate Fighting Championship

For years, Rorion Gracie had a vision of spreading the Gracie brand of Brazilian jiu-jitsu around the world. At every opportunity, he was marketing his family's martial art like Ray Kroc did with McDonald's, except in a black belt.

Never shy of the media, Rorion was known throughout the 1970s and '80s primarily for "The Gracie Challenge" in which he offered $10,000 to anyone who could defeat him in a no-holds-barred fight. In several interviews (perhaps most memorably in an issue of *Hustler* magazine, which featured a cartoon caricature of Rorion as a strutting bantam cock), he claimed to carry the $10,000 blank check with him at all times, always ready to fight anyone anywhere.

Unfortunately, while this may have scored big points with the crowds in Latin America, stories of Brazilian "death matches" over $10,000 blank checks tended to garner Rorion the sort of dubious responses normally reserved for John "Count Dante" Keehan and Guinness World Records icebreakers. For the Gracie family to gain worldwide recognition,

the challenge matches started by Maeda would have to be updated for the modern stage. Something bigger was needed. Something grander. Something … ultimate.

Enter the Octagon

In 1993, Rorion announced the formation of an event dubbed the world's first "Ultimate Fighting Championship," the first of which was took place on November 12 of that year. Fighters from a variety of martial arts styles would meet in a caged, octagon-shaped ring to compete in a "no rules" fight to the finish for a $10,000 prize.

According to Rorion, the purpose of the UFC was to act as a "laboratory" to investigate and determine, once and for all, which martial arts techniques really worked, which didn't, and which fighting style was truly the best of the best.

Among the rather motley collection of dubious "champions" supposedly representing the pinnacle of various martial arts was, not surprisingly, Royce Gracie. An accomplished fighter in his own right, Rorion's younger brother was an up-and-coming star in the world of competitive Brazilian jiu-jitsu and vale tudo.

"Ultimate" or not, "laboratory" or not, the first UFC was essentially an extension of Rorion's standing $10,000 offer—the "Gracie Challenge" in a caged octagon broadcast and brought to a pay-per-view audience.

Fittingly enough, the first UFC started with the promoter's father being awarded the title of grandmaster and ended with the promoter's brother being awarded the title of UFC champion.

Royce went on to compete in the next four UFC events, winning UFCs 1, 2 and 4. He had to drop out of the competition at the UFC 3 after a particularly grueling bout with Kimo Leopoldo. He tied Ken Shamrock at the UFC 5: Return of the Beast. Citing frustrations over new rules—especially, time limits that

he thought hindered his chances of winning— Royce left the UFC to throw down in greener pastures after the UFC 5 event.

Although the UFC would have to go on without Royce (and, ultimately, without his brother, Rorion, who later sold the promotion), the Gracie name had gained worldwide recognition, and Gracie jiu-jitsu had become the latest and greatest in cutting-edge martial arts. Across America and around the world, sensei, students and fighters flocked to "supplement" their arts with Brazilian jiu-jitsu training. Martial arts magazines were filled from cover to cover with articles about grappling, and the term "mixed martial arts"—as well as the acronym UFC—entered the national vocabulary.

As the UFC continued without the Gracies, seeing its share of both darkness (multi-state bans) to brilliance (*The Ultimate Fighter* on Spike TV's prime-time lineup every week), the MMA revolution gained speed, momentum and a power all its own—perhaps reaching a scale that even far-seeing Rorion Gracie never envisioned.

Without the Gracies, there would have been no Ultimate Fighting Championship.

Without the UFC, there would be no mixed martial arts.

Without MMA, you wouldn't be reading this book.

Next time you see a Gracie, say, "Thanks!"

HELIO GRACIE

Helio Gracie:
1997 Man of the Year

by Steve Neklia, photos by Rick Hustead
Black Belt 1997 Yearbook

The selection of *Black Belt's* 1997 Man of the Year could be viewed as more of a lifetime achievement award than as a recognition for only the past year's accomplishments. Therefore, readers should not feel bad if they are left scratching their head about this year's recipient, Helio Gracie. Although he may not be widely known in the United States, a little digging reveals that he is the man responsible for starting the grappling craze that swept the martial arts world for the past six years, a craze that is showing no signs of abating.

In his native Brazil, Helio Gracie has been a national hero and sports treasure for much of the 20th century. Born the youngest of five sons (the others being Carlos, Osvaldo, Gastão and Jorge) to Gastão and Casalina Gracie on October 1, 1913, in Belem, Para, a state in the Amazon region, Helio grew up in what was known as the Brazilian frontier. As a child, he was prone to fainting spells, and the family physician told his parents not to expose him to any physical exertion.

Around the time of Helio's birth, a Japanese fighter named Esai Maeda arrived in Brazil. Maeda's career began in wrestling contests in rural Japan. Later he studied judo and *jujutsu* and became a champion. One day, Maeda decided to

take his show on the road. He traveled the world testing his skills against those of other fighters. Eventually, he wound up in Brazil, where he fought so well that he was awarded a tract of land.

Maeda was involved in bringing Japanese settlers to Brazil. He was assisted by Helio's father, Gastão Gracie. To thank Gastão for his assistance, Maeda offered to teach jujutsu to his oldest son, Carlos Gracie.

After Carlos learned the art, the Gracie family moved to Rio de Janeiro in 1925 and opened the Academia Gracie de Jiu-Jitsu. Because Helio was weak and small, he was not permitted to participate; he had to settle for merely watching. But as he watched, he learned. He knew that he would never be able to do some of the techniques because they required too much strength. So he started altering the moves in his head, looking to exchange strength for leverage whenever possible. "I didn't invent the martial arts," he later said in an interview. "I adapted it to my necessity—what I needed for my weight and lack of strength. I learned jujutsu, but some of the moves required a lot of strength, so I could not use them. I couldn't get out from some of the positions I learned from my brother because of my lack of strength and weight, so I developed other ways out."

One day, so the story goes, Carlos was late for a jujutsu class he was supposed to teach. So Helio, who was then 16, subbed at the academy. Apparently, the students loved Helio's teaching methods so much that he decided to continue instructing.

After perfecting the Japanese way of doing jujutsu, the Gracie brothers followed in the footsteps of Maeda into the world of challenge matches. Helio soon became a standout and had very little trouble defeating all the local champions. In 1943, *Reader's Digest* published an article which claimed that a boxer had defeated a jujutsu fighter in a match intended to demonstrate the superiority of one style over another. Helio took offense at the article and approached *O Globo*, the largest newspaper in South America, to issue a challenge. He said he would make himself

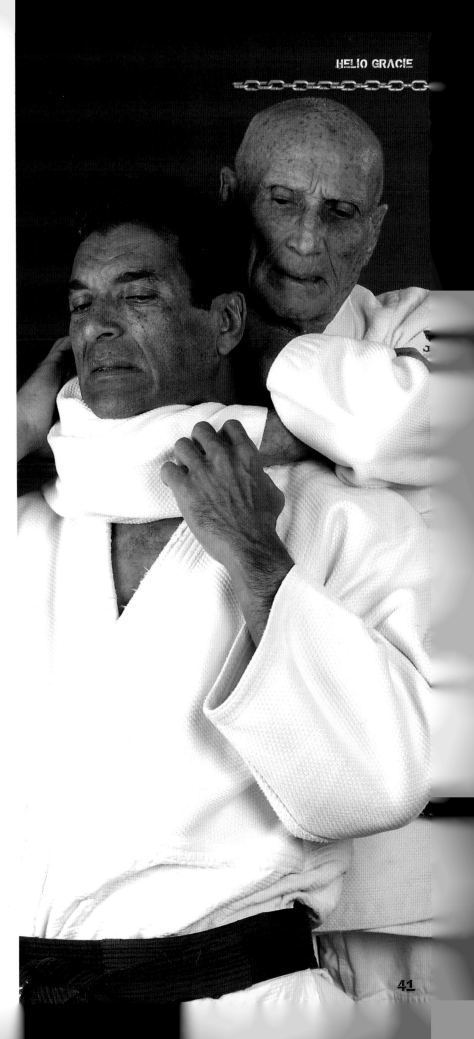

available to fight five boxers of any nationality, with or without gloves and all in the same night. He did not receive a single reply.

In 1950, boxer Joe Louis arrived in Brazil to find that Helio had sent him a telegram via *O Globo*. In part, it read: "I have just heard of the possible arrival of Joe Louis, the former heavyweight champion of the world, to our capital. I want to notify you of my disposition to face him in a match of boxing versus jujutsu to prove the superiority of the art that I practice, as well as clarify the issue of doubt raised by the magazine *Reader's Digest*." Much to Helio's disappointment, Louis never accepted the challenge.

Helio's greatest triumph in the ring may have been a 1951 loss to Masahiko Kimura, a legendary Japanese judo champ who had been undefeated for 16 years. Kimura, a much bigger and stronger man with great technique, told the press that because of the size difference, he would consider Helio the winner if he lasted longer than three minutes. Well, Helio lasted 13 minutes, and he was still fighting when Kimura caught him with an arm lock. Brother Carlos, who was afraid the technique would shatter Helio's limb, threw in the towel. Kimura was so impressed with his opponent that he invited him to teach in Japan. Luckily for Brazil, Helio declined.

Over the years, people have asked Helio why he and his family fight in challenge matches. "Because I really believe in the art," Helio answers. "How [else] could I prove it was the best art? If I say I can speak English, I need to prove

it by entering into a conversation. It's the same with the art. I believed jujutsu was the best, and if someone doubted that, I was willing to [prove it]."

Although widely known for his fighting prowess, Helio was just as revered for his teaching methods. He knew that one-on-one instruction and small classes were most beneficial to students, so that's the way jujutsu was taught. Another twist was that in his classes, the students were the ones doing the choking and the instructor was the one getting choked.

Helio devoted years to finding the best order for introducing techniques to his students. His methods became so successful that hundreds of imitators sprang up in Brazil and around the world. When asked about the differences between the Gracie family's jiu-jitsu and other styles taught in Brazil, Helio replied: "First, there are no other styles of jiu-jitsu in Brazil. The only branch in Brazil is the one that came from me. There are different scales and different levels—people who learned more and teach more efficiently and bad instructors who didn't learn from me. There are good teachers and bad teachers, but they all come from Gracie jiu-jitsu."

While the aforementioned accounts will give readers some idea of why Helio Gracie is Brazil's first and longest-reigning sports treasure, the following anecdote will help explain why he is also a national hero in that country.

In 1946, Helio and his brother were traveling to Rio de Janeiro aboard a steamer. Suddenly someone screamed, "Man overboard!" A boat full of sailors was immediately dispatched to rescue the man. The waves grew bigger as a storm approached, and the small boat had a hard time negotiating the 700 feet that lay between it and the drowning man. When the sailors finally reached the man, they struggled to pull him into the boat. They tried for 20 minutes, but the waves were so big that rescue was impossible.

The captain, fearful for the rescue crew's safety, ordered them back. In essence, he was leaving the man to die. Helio, standing on the deck of the steamer, asked his brother if he wanted to try to save the man, and his brother replied, "I don't think I can do it."

Helio then stripped to his shorts and plunged into waters he knew were shark-infested. Hoping to avoid the man-eating fish, which he predicted would be driven deeper by the storm's turbulence, he swam along the surface. On the way out, he passed the rescue crew returning to the ship. Helio ordered them to turn around again and head for the drowning man. From the water, Helio secured a hold on the floundering man, and with the help of the sailors, Helio yanked him into the boat, thus saving his life.

Brazil presented Helio Gracie with the medal of honor for his bravery. *Black Belt* presents him with its Man of the Year award for his outstanding contribution to the martial arts.

For more information, visit www.gracieacademy.com.

LET A NEW ADVENTURE BEGIN

by Edward Pollard
Black Belt May 2009

News of Helio Gracie's death on January 29, 2009, spread rapidly in the martial arts community and was soon all over the Internet, from mainstream Web sites to small-time blogs. In keeping with Brazilian tradition, the 95-year-old patriarch was interred within 24 hours, hardly enough time for anyone but nearby family and friends to attend the burial. He'd been at his ranch in Itaipava, a town near Petropolis, north of Rio de Janeiro, known for its natural beauty and cultural attractions. It's a fitting point of departure for a man whose age and activity level were rivaled only by Jack LaLanne, who's still alive and kicking at 94. Gracie probably exercised more in his later years than the average American teenager in the peak of youth.

The fifth and youngest son of Gastão Gracie, Helio embodied Gracie *jiu-jitsu* in professional and challenge matches from the 1930s to the 1960s, long before his eldest son Rorion Gracie brought it to Southern California and co-founded the Ultimate Fighting Championship. Helio faced men much larger than himself just to prove that the system he devised was effective, that it gave a smaller, weaker man the advantage when used intelligently. It was the art of the underdog honed to perfection.

To honor his accomplishments, a memorial celebration took place at the Gracie Jiu-Jitsu Academy in Torrance, California, on February 7, 2009. From the outside, there were no visible signs that anything special was happening—no valets, banners, signs, buntings or balloons. The lobby was quiet, and only a few people sat on the sofas. Several children wandered about. When I rounded the corner near the main training area, however, I saw a crowd of 200 standing and sitting around a small stage with what amounted to an open mike.

Rorion and sons Ryron and Rener shared emcee duties, inviting family members, students and friends up to recount memories of their venerated elder. This is how I learned that, aside from having effectively redesigned Japanese *jujutsu*, Helio considered himself the best driver in Brazil. In his opinion, anyone who stepped on the brake pedal was lacking some necessary skills. As a parental authority figure, he instilled a certain respectful fear in his progeny because he missed nothing. His second son Relson shared a long anecdote about having a counterfeit school stamp made so he could skip classes in favor of surfing and playing soccer. The ruse worked for six months, he said, until the school contacted his father. The punishment? Six months of house arrest and homework.

Ryron spoke enthusiastically about his grandfather's influence: "I don't think he truly realized how big the revolution that he caused was and how many lives he impacted. What he did know about it made him very happy, content and fully at ease. He realized his mission. As a result, I think our family could deal with it a lot easier than most because we knew that he couldn't have been happier. It was time to go."

Rorion hovered near the stage, always ready to keep the energy level high and the focus on his father. He made sure that those assembled never felt that it was anything but a tribute to the glorious deeds of an unlikely hero.

"Isn't that interesting that a person in his influential position, who touched so many people, taught us another lesson in passing away?" he said. "Not only we who grew up with him, and who learned to see things in a certain way, but everybody else, as well. All I'm trying to do is take it as lightly and happily as he would wish us to do. I'm extremely fortunate that I had the opportunity to do everything I did for the old man. If he were 100 or 120 years old, eventually he'd have to go. He passed the torch, and now we're carrying on. Changing worlds is a good thing; it's not a bad thing. But he believed in reincarnation anyway. He's probably around here somewhere now, growing up and choking people out."

I had the chance to ask another veteran grappler his opinion of the elder martial artist's passing—at 76, the comparatively young Gene LeBell.

"Helio was an icon in the martial arts, and he will be missed, but what he did will live on in his students," LeBell said. "His kids gave him a lot of respect. When Royce entered an arena, they all came in a line with their hands on each other's shoulders, and the old man was right in there. He couldn't have weighed 130 pounds, but he adapted jiu-jitsu for everybody and was a very good teacher who lasted a long time. I give him a lot of credit for that—and for sky diving when he was very old."

It's been said that after you depart this mortal plane, all that's left is a dash between two dates. For most of us, that may be true. We may leave behind a child or two, a smidgen of property if we worked hard and made careful life choices, and that's about it. From age 16, Helio Gracie put his stamp on an entire martial art, changed its course and cleared the way for a new sport that outgrew his influence but not his legacy. It's a footprint that spans continents and cultures.

For more information, visit www.gracieacademy.com.

KYRA GRACIE

Up Close and Personal With Kyra Gracie

Meet the Newest Star of the Legendary Brazilian Grappling Family!

by the Editors of Black Belt, photos by Rick Hustead
Black Belt June 2008

You could safely say that there's no martial artist in the West who hasn't heard the name "Gracie"—whether it's attached to Rickson, Royce, Rorion, Renzo, Ralph, Royler or Carlson; to one of Brazilian *jiu-jitsu's* patriarchs, Helio and Carlos Sr.; or to one of the up-and-coming fighters like Ralek and Ryron. Obviously, the family has left an indelible mark on the modern history of the martial arts. Noticeably absent from that list, however, is the name of even one woman. That's because, in the rough-and-tumble world of grappling, Gracie girls are practically nonexistent.

Enter Kyra Gracie, the woman who won the 132-pound division at the 2007 Abu Dhabi Combat Club Submission Wrestling World Championships. The Brazilian native is now based in Southern California, and she has big plans to increase the number of women participating in jiu-jitsu around the world. We expect to see a lot more of her in the future as her skills develop and her competition career continues, so we're offering the following as an introduction.

KYRA GRACIE

Age: 22

Marital status: single

Place of birth: Rio de Janeiro

Mother: Flavia Gracie

Famous uncles: Ralph Gracie, Renzo Gracie

Grandfather: Robson Gracie

Date of arrival in the United States: 2005

Place of residence: Irvine, California

Hobbies: jiu-jitsu, traveling, spending time at the beach

Dojo at which she teaches: "I don't teach regularly, but I do seminars on the weekends."

Rank: black belt

Date of promotion to black belt: 2006

Promoted by: Carlos Gracie Jr. of Gracie Barra

Current instructor: Carlos Gracie Jr. "But I also have the pleasure of training with other members of my family, such as Renzo and Rilion."

Years she won the Abu Dhabi Combat Club Submission Wrestling World Championships: 2005, 2007 "They just started having the ADCC for women

Years she won the World Brazilian Jiu-Jitsu Championship: 2004, 2006

Years she won the Pan-American Brazilian Jiu-Jitsu Games: 2001, 2002, 2003, 2005, 2007

Next tournament on her agenda: World Brazilian Jiu-Jitsu Championship in June 2008

Favorite technique: omo plata

Favorite Brazilian jiu-jitsu competitor: Roger Gracie

Favorite Ultimate Fighting Championship fighter: Antonio Rodrigo "Minotauro" Nogueira

Prospects for ever fighting in a mixed-martial arts match: "Maybe yes, maybe no."

Martial arts goal: "To get more women involved in Brazilian jiu-jitsu."

Family's reaction when she decided to compete: "In the beginning, it was tough because a lot of my family is old-fashioned and didn't think a girl should be doing this, but now they all support me."

—Editors of *Black Belt*

RALEK GRACIE

Growing Up Gracie

by Edward Pollard, photos by Rick Hustead
Black Belt March 2008

It isn't every day that you get to sit down and pick the brain of a member of a martial arts dynasty. If any patronymic has ever embodied the concept of dynasty in its field of influence, the Gracie name is it. Ralek Gracie is the son of Rorion, the man who co-founded the Ultimate Fighting Championship in 1993 when Ralek was only 8. You have to wonder what it's like to grow up in a family that big and that influential in the martial arts and even in popular culture. How does it shape the way you see the world? How does the world appear when you're on the inside looking out?

Q: You just won an important bout in K-1 HERO's. Was that your first big public fight?
A: That was my first fight, amateur or professional.

Q: How long did you train for it?
A: Honestly, I've been training my whole life for that fight, but specifically, I knew three weeks in advance. I knew who my opponent was, and I trained specifically for this person, but the training never really stops.

Q: Who trained and cornered you?
A: I had two of my good training partners, Jared Quity and Kevin Casey. Kevin trains out of Rickson Gracie's academy. I thought it was good to get some of Rickson's ideas into the whole thing because I definitely respect him as a fighter.

Q: What's your weight class, and is it close to your walking-around weight?
A: I fought at 205, light-heavyweight, but most likely I'm going to be fighting at 185 for the next one. My walking-around weight is closer to 210 or 215.

Q: Was it a lot of work to get down to middleweight?
A: Not really. In two weeks of training hard, I cut weight like you wouldn't believe.

Q: Did the bout go as expected?
A: It went according to plan, more than I thought it would. I slipped on the mat at the beginning, lost my footing and fell over, but I quickly regained my balance and continued the fight. I didn't know what the ring felt like. The day of the fight, I felt the ring and moved around a little bit, but it's not really enough time to get accustomed to that kind of mat.

Q: How do you feel about your title chances?
A: At this point, I'm just trying to get comfortable in the ring. Once I do that, I'll set my sights on whoever's on top at the time.

Q: Do you know who your next opponent might be?
A: They want me to fight Mike Tyson. (laughs) No, definitely not. I'm just trying to put it out there. I would definitely take that fight, but that's not what they want. Honestly, I don't know who my next opponent might be.

Q: Do you see any specific mixed-martial arts skill areas that aren't covered by Gracie *jiu-jitsu*?
A: As far as cross-training in general, I think training in *muay Thai* or any kind of stand-up will always improve your chances of taking a punch and understanding punch defense and also hitting somebody. You definitely should be as well-rounded as you can be. I prefer muay Thai and trained at Fairtex for a while. The guys are good over there. I think jiu-jitsu alone can take any style and is No. 1. It can also compete in MMA alone. However, I believe that it's good for a fighter to know as much as he can when he steps into the ring. If you're a black belt in kung fu, great; use that to be a better fighter. Do whatever you can to be your best. That's my philosophy.

Q: What's it like growing up in the Gracie family?
A: Interesting. Crazy. There were many altercations—in a friendly way, though. While growing up, my brothers and I would always push it to the limit. We would check each other and test each other. I was always there to bug my brothers just to get a rise out of them. There were five of us in the house: my two older brothers, my younger brother and my younger sister. It was chaos. Everybody was just running around. Somebody would get choked out or tackled. But the respect was always there. We respected our elders. I learned quickly that I had to respect my older brothers and my dad.

Q: What was it like being a Gracie on the playground? Did it have repercussions?
A: No. Of course, people know that you're a Gracie, and they look at you, but they always think twice because they've seen the UFC and what Royce did to people twice his size. I did get tested. I would use my jiu-jitsu in a different way. I'd try to help the kid who couldn't defend himself. In the event that I would fight, I'd try to control the person and not pummel his face and make him bleed. My father used to say that controlling someone makes him feel the same as if you beat him to a pulp. He's going to feel dominated, and you'll win. When you're in fifth grade and you just hold a kid down, it's much more serious to him.

Q: Are there more advantages or disadvantages to having the family name?
A: It's a gift and a curse all the way. People think: "If I beat him, I'm moving up. If I lose to him, oh, I lost to a Gracie—no big deal." OK, you can win, but we're just going to keep coming. We don't stop.

Q: Do you feel extra pressure to live up to the reputation?
A: It helps me train harder than a lot of people. It helps me stay mentally [tough]. I have to be able to win fights and keep doing what the family's done for decades.

The family tradition is imbedded in me. I want to keep a strong name in the MMA game. Every eight seconds there's a Gracie being born around the world. You can't run no matter what.

Q: Who else in your family, besides your father, do you rely on to help you make important decisions about your career?
A: Royce. I trust and respect his opinion. He's been around since the days when he and my father were teaching out of his garage. He's very close to me. He's almost like a dad because he was always there for me. I have pictures of him holding me when I was 2.

Q: What are your goals as an athlete, and as a Gracie?

A: I want to keep the sound of the Gracie name in the MMA ear worldwide. I want to take it into different areas and do new things with the Gracie name.

Q: Like what?
A: I want to have a Gracie toaster. You know it's going to be a strong toaster and it will last long. It's going to have longevity and really cook things. That's metaphorically speaking. It could be anything. If something has the Gracie name on it, it has tradition, values, strength and dignity—all good qualities that we want in everything. Right now, I'm working on my clothing line, Ralek Gracie Apparel, and my Web site, www.ralekgracie.tv.

RENZO GRACIE

Profile: Renzo Gracie

by Jason William McNeil, photos by Tiago Molinos
BOOK EXCLUSIVE

Brazilian Fighting Tradition

To say it wasn't easy growing up Gracie would be to indulge in the depths of understatement. Like all the male members of Brazil's sprawling and spreading Gracie clan, Renzo Gracie was practically raised on the judo mats, rolling and wrestling with his father, uncles and brothers

before he was even old enough to walk.

The Gracie men are fighters, pure and simple. Their combative skills—descended from Japanese samurai and filtered through the rough-and-tumble world of Latin American wrestling and bare-knuckle brawling—have been honed into one of the world's most famous and feared fighting styles.

Being a Gracie man comes with a legacy to uphold. For Renzo, the Gracie name brings with it both responsibility and opportunity: the responsibility to live up to the standards set by the world's most famous fighting family, and the opportunity to add to the legacy—to let the Gracie *jiu-jitsu* passed down from generation to generation lead him around the world, from country to country, from arena to arena, and from victory to victory.

For Renzo Gracie, his family name isn't just something he has to live up to. It's a legacy he's intent on leaving greater and more illustrious than he found it. Rather than worry about how high his brethren have set the bar, Renzo is determined to raise it even higher.

Get in the Ring!

As one expects of Gracie men, Renzo carried the family honor into the ring, willing to prove to any and all comers that his expression of Brazilian jiu-jitsu was a fighting force to be feared and reckoned with.

In 1992, more than two years before the Ultimate Fighting Championship began its onslaught of the martial arts world at large, Renzo first entered the professional fighting world at the Desafio-Gracie *vale tudo* event, facing down and defeating Luiz Augusto Alvareda seven minutes into the first round. It was an auspicious start to what would go on to be a Gracie-worthy fighting career.

Renzo's early notable victories also included an impressive three wins against three opponents in a single night at the World Combat Championship 1: First Strike eight-man elimination tournament in 1995, and his 1996 knockout of the UFC 6's tournament champion, Oleg Taktarov, at MARS: Martial Arts Reality Superfighting.

(There was also Renzo's interesting match for the Pentagon Combat promotion, which was officially ruled a no contest when the event had to be called on account of fan rioting. Ah, the exciting early days of mixed-martial arts events.)

Gracie PRIDE

Following his handy defeat of Taktarov, and sporting an impressive 5-0 professional record, Renzo accepted an offer to fight for the fledgling Japanese-based fight promotion PRIDE. It would be the beginning of a long run with PRIDE that would encompass many of the most memorable fights of his career.

At the first PRIDE Fighting Championships, Renzo helped inaugurate the promotion by battling Japanese fighter Akira Shoji for a full half-hour (divided into three rounds). Neither fighter was able to gain a clear upper hand, and the bout was declared a draw.

Returning for PRIDE 2, Renzo seemed determined not to leave room for any ambiguity of decision. Trading locks and licks with another Japanese fighter, Sanae Kikuta, for nearly an hour, Renzo finally choked out his opponent in the middle of their sixth grueling 10-minute round.

Clearly, Renzo had come to Japan to fight.

It's been observed that nothing succeeds like success, and Renzo seemed positively flushed with success in the Land of the Rising Sun. At PRIDE 8, he beat Alexander Otsuka via judges' decision and, just a month later, battled his way to victories over Wataru Sakata and Maurice Smith (the first ever kickboxer to win the UFC 14: Showdown) in a single night at the RINGs King of Kings tournament. In the 2000 King of Kings quarterfinals, however, Renzo lost a tough decision to Kiyoshi Timura.

Less than a year later, Renzo returned to the Wild East for PRIDE 10: Return of the Warriors to face the Japanese "Gracie Killer," Kazushi Sakuraba. Before his match with Renzo, Sakuraba had already famously defeated both Royler Gracie and three-time UFC titleholder Royce Gracie, so it was with a certain amount of determination to

avenge the family honor that Renzo climbed into the ring.

Amazingly, Renzo refused to tap out even after Sakuraba had dislocated his elbow. The Brazilian insisted that he could still beat the Japanese fighter even with one useless arm, but the referee disagreed and stopped the fight, awarding yet another Gracie head to the "Gracie Killer."

Renzo's slump continued through PRIDE 13: Collision Course, in which he suffered a nasty knockout loss to Dan Henderson early in the first round.

Renzo seemed set to return to his winning ways with a defeat of Michiyoshi Ohara at 2001's PRIDE 17: Championship Chaos, but everything began to unravel the following year with heartbreakingly close losses via decision to Shungo Oyama at PRIDE 21: Demolition and via split decision to Carlos Newton at 2003's PRIDE: Bushido 1. Following the Newton loss, Renzo no longer fought for the PRIDE organization but continued to appear in a promotional capacity as a commentator and occasional interviewee.

Grudge Match

Renzo's first post-PRIDE matchup would mark the beginning of what became his most famous rivalry.

B.J. Penn was, by all accounts, an impressive young fighter who had been schooled in the art of Brazilian jiu-jitsu by Renzo's brother, Ralph Gracie. Apparently, Ralph had been impressed with the brawling Hawaiian's fighting spirit and had personally taken Penn under his wing to teach him the secrets of Gracie jiu-jitsu.

As with most other martial traditions, one of the central tenants of Gracie jiu-jitsu is loyalty to the style and, by extension, to the Gracie family. Therefore, it's perhaps understandable that the Gracies took particular umbrage at Penn's

abruptly leaving the style and subsequently attacking specific Gracies—in what they perceived to be blatant self-service to his career.

In 2005, B.J. Penn violated all Gracie jiu-jitsu tradition by publicly "calling out" (challenging) the venerated Rodrigo Gracie.

"B.J. was one of the best fighters we (the Gracies) ever produced," Renzo says. "And then, one day, he just flipped and changed teams."

Following Penn's victory via decision over Rodrigo, every Gracie worth his salt was gunning for the upstart. When Penn's next public calling out was directed at his teacher's own brother (as well as being Rodrigo's cousin), Renzo was only too happy to answer the challenge.

He was not at all happy, however, about the way the challenge was issued. "I was in Best Buy, buying a new iPod, and my phone rang," Renzo explains. "It was B.J.'s father—not B.J. but his *father*—calling me to fight him. I had had a little altercation in the street … I had to hold this kid down, and when I held him down, my kneecap snapped. So that's why it took me a long time to heal enough to be healthy enough to fight again. So I got this call … it could be anybody, but it was his father!"

As he continues the story, it's clear that this particular subject is one that sets Renzo's Brazilian blood boiling. "That was the biggest insult of my life!" Renzo fumes. "If I'm going to call someone to fight me, I'll call him myself, not have my father call for me. To me, that means he's calling for his son because he's sure he's going to beat me up! Even though I was still hurt, I told him I'd take the fight anyway. I was so mad. The only thing I was thinking is I'll leave a very good shot in his face—that round, ugly face that he has!"

Frustratingly for Renzo, the two fought viciously to a very close decision at K-1's World Grand Prix Hawaii in July 2005, but Penn narrowly edged out the victory.

"After the air was cleared and all was said and done, we've got no more problems, really," Renzo explains. "That's why fighting is sometimes the best thing. We settled the challenge."

Renzo readily admits, "B.J. was the toughest fight I ever had. It was like fighting myself. He trained in our style, fights my style, so he was really my toughest opponent."

The Gracies ultimately achieved some measure of satisfaction when their star student, Georges St. Pierre, finally defeated Penn via decision at the UFC 58.

Master of the Flying Guillotine!

After taking a year off to train and regroup, Renzo returned to his winning ways with a flying guillotine choke victory over former UFC welterweight titleholder Pat Miletich in the first round of IFL: Gracie vs. Miletich in September 2006.

Renzo was back on his game. More wins followed, including a particularly satisfying rematch victory over Newton at the International Fighting League's Championship Final and a knock-down, drag-out fight with former UFC champ Frank Shamrock at EliteXC: Destiny in February 2007, which ended with Shamrock's disqualification for repeated knee strikes to the back of the head. Battered and bruised, both fighters were helped from the ring.

Now in his early 40s, Renzo trains others to fight more than he fights himself, both at his own gym in New York City and at seminars around the world (including an annual appearance in Virginia at Radford University's Karate College, where the gregarious coach trains hundreds of up-and-comers over the course of a four-day summer weekend), but he still doesn't consider himself "retired." He says he plans to get back in the ring soon and that he's just looking for the right opportunity to present itself.

With Shamrock a weekly feature on the NBC network's Strikeforce, might a Renzo-vs.-Shamrock rematch be just the ticket to pull Renzo back into competition?

One can only hope, watch and wait.

In the meantime, Holmdel, New Jersey's most famous Brazilian transplant will continue to train, continue to travel, and continue to do his part to spread the good news of the Gracie jiu-jitsu

gospel to anyone who's willing to learn what he has to teach.

If you want to walk the path the Gracies have blazed, Renzo is more than willing to be your guide. Just do him (and yourself) a favor and respect the family traditions. Not only is Renzo one of the best fighters to come out of Brazil—and, therefore, not someone you want to have annoyed with you—but he's also got an awful lot of brothers ... and cousins ... and uncles ... and children ... and even his daughters' boyfriends, it seems.

The Gracies have firmly established themselves as the first family of mixed martial arts. For all they've done and continue to do, they deserve nothing but respect.

And they'll accept nothing less.

RORION GRACIE

Latest News From the Birthplace of Brazilian Jiu-Jitsu in America

By Edward Pollard, photos by Rick Hustead
Black Belt December 2006

It's been 20 years since the Gracie name started making waves in the American martial arts community and 13 since Royce Gracie first demonstrated the art at the Ultimate Fighting Championship. After a string of wins, the disap- pointments began as several family members fell to cross-training opponents. It seemed like years passed with nary a peep from the Gracies—until Royce entered the octagon to face Matt Hughes. And we all know how that ended.

Yet on Rorion Gracie's side of the family, business is better than ever. With the blessing of his father Helio Gracie, Rorion and his sons have continued to run the *jiu-jitsu* academy that's stood on Carson Street in Torrance, California, for the past 16 years. They've refined what they're offering the public, and they've brainstormed a bunch of new products *Black Belt* readers are sure to be interested in. The update follows.

Q: What's the big news in the Gracie empire?
Rorion Gracie: We're getting ready to move the academy to a new location after 16 years. Our Internet business has grown a lot, so we need a storage and shipping area that can accommodate the demand.

Q: Where will the new academy be located?
Rorion: Five minutes north of where we are now—literally 30 seconds off the 405 freeway. It's much more accessible for everyone. It's going to be the most amazing martial arts school of all time. Our Web site will remain the same—www. gracie.com. I had to say that. (laughs)

Q: Are there any new features on your Web site?
Ralek Gracie: We just came out with a monthly newsletter, *Gracie Insider*. We're trying to keep people up to date with snippets of my brothers and me around the academy and information on techniques that we discovered and want to show people.

Q: Do you have any new DVDs in the works?
Rorion: We're releasing instructional DVDs that are revised versions of the videotapes that I did with Royce years ago.

Q: What are the differences between the originals and the revamped versions?
Rorion: The content of the DVDs is the same as the old instructional tapes, but they have special, never-seen bonus footage of my sons Ryron and Rener giving tips on grappling and jiu-jitsu techniques. They're amazing techniques, very

well-presented. There are [pointers on] what your state of mind should be when you're training. We also have a guided tour of the Gracie museum, which is a special bonus feature for people around the world who've never had a chance to visit it. I present the tour and talk about the history of the Gracie family.

Q: Is there anything more you'd care to say about the DVDs?
Rorion: There are four different sets to the Gracie DVD collection: the basics, the intermediate [course], the advanced [course] and street self-defense. People who buy the complete collection will get 50-year-old archival footage of my father and my Uncle Carlos, a movie I thought was destroyed. I took it to a lab in Hollywood, and they were able to recover this stuff from the ashes. And before I forget, we now have *Gracie Jiu-jitsu in Action, Volume 1* and *Volume 2* available on UMD for the Sony PlayStation Portable.

Q: Is there a Gracie video game?
Rorion: Not yet. It's all part of the project. First things first.

Q: Have you designed any new apparel?
Rorion: My sons have designed a line of clothing. They've come up with a very interesting concept called the Submission Series, which is the seven most common submission techniques used in Gracie jiu-jitsu. Each design features not only the move itself but also an explanation of what it's called, the consequences if it's applied on someone, and a philosophical and practical breakdown of the move—all of which is printed on a shirt.

Q: So someone standing behind you in line at the movie theater …
Rorion: … Is reading about the arm lock, yes.

Q: It sounds like a clever way to use what is typically treated as ad space.
Rorion: They're very popular T-shirts. We have

four of the seven available. These guys are always coming up with new looks for shirts and stuff like that. We have a variety of clothing for different occasions—such as fight shorts that you can grapple or surf or swim in.

Ralek: You'll be seeing us wearing the fight shorts soon in the octagon.

Q: Ralek, are you going to fight soon?

Ralek: We're constantly training—it's just a matter of everything coming together and finding the right time. Of course, my brothers and I are getting more involved in the business—teaching, designing clothing and, for Rener, running the Web site—but we also have to train to stay on top of the game. More than anything, our goal is eventually to go in there and challenge the current people. Before that, we have a lot of missions to make happen.

Q: Your family has obviously experienced plenty of success in mixed martial arts. It seems as though there's nothing left to prove.

Ralek: It's just a matter of competing for ourselves. I enjoy fighting; it's something I wake up thinking about. Aside from that, it's about accomplishing more for the overall movement of Gracie jiu-jitsu.

Rorion: The essence of this movement is to educate as many people as possible about the benefits of knowing Gracie jiu-jitsu. It's something that gives a person a lot of tranquility and confidence, and that can affect life in a whole bunch of

ways, much more than knowing how to fight. It makes an attorney a better attorney, a doctor a better doctor, an engineer a better engineer—all because they acquire confidence from Gracie jiu-jitsu.

Q: Confidence and self-esteem are important foundations in everyone's life.
Rorion: They did so much for my dad at 140 pounds back in Brazil that he embraced the Gracie cause of making that available for as many people as possible. That's what brought me to America, and these boys are carrying on the mission of making sure that the techniques and teachings are accessible to as many people as possible all over the world. That's the plan.

Q: What else have you been doing to further your goal of spreading jiu-jitsu?
Rorion: In October 2003, the U.S. Army officially adopted Gracie jiu-jitsu for its combatives program. Now they're unfolding it on a larger scale. It's officially part of [the training at] Fort Benning [Georgia]. We're continually traveling and certifying military instructors so they can pass the information on to other soldiers. It's been very successful because the Army is not only about shooting. Sometimes they have to shoot, sometimes they have to separate [members of opposing political or religious groups] and sometimes they have to give humanitarian aid. They just can't go in with guns and start shooting people. When they need an intermediate solution, Gracie jiu-jitsu allows them to control the situation without having to kill anyone.

Q: Training for up-close situations is important in law enforcement, too.
Rorion: That's why our program is so popular within the law-enforcement community. Everybody from the Secret Service and FBI to the DEA and Homeland Security—all regularly send their [agents] to our school.

Q: Most martial artists would have trouble handling all those projects.
Rorion: They keep us quite busy. We're also getting materials ready for the next book. We're doing a photographic essay of the Gracie family's history—newspaper clippings and photos and stuff like that. And we're co-producing a documentary on these boys.

Q: Have any new celebrities started training at the Gracie Jiu-Jitsu Academy?
Rorion: Dr. Robert Rey from *Dr. 90210* has decided to return to his roots—he's Brazilian—and take jiu-jitsu. He's doing very well. Ed O'Neill from *Married With Children* continues to choke us out regularly. People like Nicolas Cage, Michael Clarke Duncan and Shaquille O'Neal have experienced jiu-jitsu and understand what the mechanics are. They're strong supporters of the whole thing.

BB: How do you train a guy the size of Shaq?
Ralek: Just feed him the basics—that's all he needs. His strength and size carry him the rest of the way.

Royce Gracie

The man who changed the world: Fifteen years after the UFC was conceived, Royce Gracie looks back at how his fighting art rocked the martial arts!

by Robert W. Young, photos by Rick Hustead
Black Belt January 2008

Where were you 15 years ago? According to the most recent *Black Belt* reader survey, many of you weren't into the martial arts yet. Some of you weren't even born. If you fall into either category, it means that everything you know about the arts has been shaped to some extent by the accomplishments of a single man: Royce Gracie.

Let's journey back to the pre-Royce era for a moment. When it came to realistic combat, kickboxing was king. Nowhere else could a fighter throw full-power kicks and punches and, if Thai rules were used, elbows and knees.

When it came to cross-training, multiculturalism was it. Practitioners loved to tell people things like, "I do the Korean arts for kicking, the Japanese arts for punching, the Philippine arts for weapons and the Indonesian arts for close-range combat."

When it came to sheer, unadulterated toughness, the Sabaki Challenge and the Shidokan Open were on top. Their bone-breaking bare-knuckle bouts were the domain of karate's baddest dudes.

Then, in early 1993, Rorion Gracie and Art Davie hatched a plan for a new test of combat skills. Dubbed the Ultimate Fighting Championship, it would pit practitioners of a variety of martial arts against one another in a three-tiered tournament. The winner of the first event, held in late 1993, as well as the second event and a couple of big bouts afterward, was Royce. Single-handedly, he established the Gracie name in America and around the world. In doing so, he redefined realistic combat, cross-training and our concept of toughness.

Black Belt caught up with Royce, now 40, in between seminar tours and pelted him with questions about his family's style of *jiu-jitsu*, his life after the UFC and his role in changing the history of the martial arts.

Q: It's nearly 15 years after the Ultimate Fighting Championship began. In your view, how did your performance in its first few shows affect the martial arts world?
A: Now everybody knows jiu-jitsu. The same way that all the grapplers learned that they have to incorporate some type of stand-up martial arts like boxing or kickboxing—even if they don't use it—the stand-up guys learned that they have to incorporate some type of grappling. That grappling is usually Gracie jiu-jitsu. It was a big eye-opener for the martial arts world.

Q: When you began winning, the first reaction of many martial artists was denial. Then it seemed as though they relented and reluctantly studied jiu-jitsu. What about now? Are they still learning it because they have to, or are they actually eager to pick up ground skills?
A: When the UFC started, many people didn't even consider grappling a martial art. Many times since then, I've had grapplers come up to me and say, "Thanks for putting us on the map." Today, everyone wants to learn some type of grappling. If they cannot get their hands on Gracie jiu-jitsu, they settle for judo or wrestling or something along those lines.

They realize that grappling is important to know in case they go to the ground in a fight.

If you can knock a guy out with one punch and the fight is over, perfect. That's a beautiful fight. But if the guy is bigger and stronger and can absorb your punch, you've got to take him to the ground and choke him out. That's what we've always taught.

Q: How widespread is the popularity of Brazilian jiu-jitsu?
A: I do seminars around the world. The average number of people at each one is 40 to 50, which is a lot. I normally spend about 15 days at home with my family and 15 days on the road teaching, and I'm booked far in advance. Jiu-jitsu's popularity is definitely growing.

Q: Which group is your favorite to teach: military, police, civilians? ...
A: Civilians. You can see it in their eyes when they learn something new. They're like, Why didn't I think of that? Especially beginners—they really appreciate the techniques they're learning.

Q: These days, would it be fair to say that every mixed-martial arts fighter knows Brazilian jiu-jitsu?
A: Even if they don't do it, they know some of the techniques. Even people who do judo and wrestling learn Gracie jiu-jitsu. Once they learn it, they combine the moves with their own style.

Q: What about world-class wrestlers? Isn't their style of grappling enough for the ground portion of MMA fighting?
A: In wrestling, you don't have submissions. Wrestling is enough to take a guy down and control him, but then what do you do? Let the guy get back up and do it again and hope to win by points? What if you face a guy who offers some resistance and won't let you take him down? What if you get only one chance to take him down? Maybe you could finish it with a submission then and there. Jiu-jitsu is an excellent supplement for every style out there.

Q: If a fighter adopts Brazilian jiu-jitsu as his base, what skills would you recommend he augment it with for use in MMA?
A: Thai boxing. I'm a big fan of Thai boxing. I go to Fairtex quite a bit, and they help me a lot. It's the best striking style for MMA because it teaches elbows and knees. They also do takedowns such as the foot sweep.

Q: Is a combination of Brazilian jiu-jitsu and Thai boxing the best for self-defense, too?
A: Gracie jiu-jitsu is enough for self-defense. We cover escapes from every position that you can imagine. If you're talking about an MMA fight, however, it's a different story.

Q: How has your family's art changed over the past 15 years?
A: A perfect example comes from Ralek Gracie, my nephew. He had a fight in K-1 HERO's in July 2007. He used a side kick, got in a clinch, took his opponent down and mounted him before going for the arm lock. I think he used a couple of hits to soften the guy up first. It was a classic fight even though it was from a kid who's 22 years old and part of a new generation of up-and-coming fighters. The basics of jiu-jitsu don't change. The strategy—how you approach the fight—might change, but the foundation of the house is the same.

Q: MMA competition has evolved away from the use of uniforms. When you teach these days, do you focus more on no-*gi* training?
A: No. Most of my seminars are with a gi. My law-enforcement seminars are no-gi, of course. I do a lot of gi training when I work out. If I'm preparing for a fight in America, I train no-gi because we're not allowed to wear a gi. But if I'm training just to train—to roll around—I prefer to wear a gi because you have more tools to play with. It's like boxing, in which you can use only your hands, versus *muay Thai*, in which you can use your hands, feet, elbows and knees. When you have more tools to use,

it becomes more fun. No-gi fighting has a very limited number of chokes and locks.

Q: When you started competing in the UFC, Brazilian jiu-jitsu fighters could win with just the basics. But now, it seems as though it takes a higher level of technique to win. What's changed?
A: It's still classic jiu-jitsu. The difference is that some fighters are more aware of what's coming, so they hide their arms. When they do that, you have to go for a choke or a foot lock. You have to keep changing to find the opening, instead of just going for one technique and running the risk that they'll block it.

Q: Do you also try to create openings?
A: You have to do that, too. You cannot depend on them feeding you something. You've got to put a lot of things out there to get them to leave an opening.

Q: How good are the Brazilian jiu-jitsu skills we see in MMA nowadays? Are they high level, or are the fighters successful only because they're combining so-so jiu-jitsu with decent kickboxing skills?
A: The fighters are very skilled. Most of the ones from Brazil have won world championships. The problem is, there's no money in jiu-jitsu competition. They get to a certain point in their life and decide they need to make money. That's why they enter MMA.

Q: Who are the best American fighters out there now?
A: Randy Couture is definitely a tough cookie. I'm an old man, too, so he's my kind of guy. Chuck Liddell is also a great fighter. He's had a couple of tough matches and just has to put

his head back in the game. There are lots of good guys—it's hard to name all of them.

Q: Which MMA athlete do you most like to watch? Who's the most entertaining?
A: The Chute Boxe guys. They either do the knockout or get knocked out. You never see a boring fight from them.

Q: Do you have any students who are rising through the MMA ranks?
A: Buddy Clinton. He fights for King of the Cage. He hasn't won a title yet, but after a couple of wins, he's ready for a shot at the title.

Q: Are the skills you teach students like Clinton the same as what you taught 15 years ago?
A: The foundation is the same. After you build the foundation, the student has to add his personal style.

Q: What are the most common mistakes you see as you conduct your seminars?
A: People trying to take shortcuts. Instead of going from one to two to three, sometimes they think, I want to go from one to three to make it faster. But when they do that, they lose the technique. I tell them to slow down. Speed comes with time. Strength you add later.

Q: Say a person wants to be an MMA fighter. What advice would you give him with respect to techniques, conditioning and strength?
A: First, to win a fight, you've got to know what you're doing. If you don't know what you're doing, you have no reason to be in the ring. Second, you can have the fastest or most powerful car in the world, but if it doesn't have any gas, you're not going anyplace. You've got to fill up the tank—that's techniques. Then comes strength. So it goes in that order: You've got to know what you're doing and have the techniques, then develop the conditioning and strength.

Q: After that, is it a matter of gaining experience, of working your way up?
A: You can try to take a shortcut, but in the end you've got to build a reputation. A lot of guys think, I'm not going to fight unless I get a shot at the title. But who the heck are they? They have to prove themselves before they get to fight the champ.

Q: How long should an aspiring fighter expect to compete before he makes money?
A: If a guy steps into the ring, he should get paid. But there's a ranking. If you build your way up and fight the top guys, you should get more money. If you fight no-names, you get paid less. That's the nature of the business.

Q: When is your next fight?
A: I'm getting too old for this. (laughs) Once a year is plenty for me. My next fight won't be until next year.

Q: When you're training for a fight, what's a typical week like?
A: Monday through Saturday, I do 45 minutes to an hour of stand-up—mostly muay Thai—and 45 minutes to an hour of grappling. I also lift weights three or four days a week. Conditioning I do 50 minutes to an hour three or four days a week. I might put a couple of runs in, no more than four miles, in the sand on the beach.

Q: What's the biggest project on the horizon for you?
A: Right now, I'm concentrating on teaching and conducting seminars. I'm very busy with that. My biggest project, though, is taking care of my family and raising my four kids.

FORREST GRIFFIN

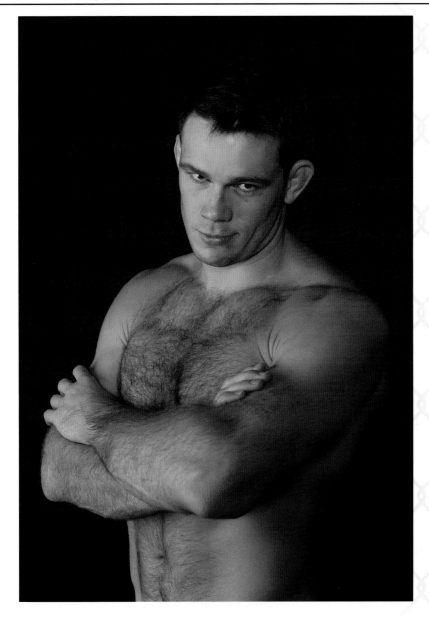

Q & A With Forrest Griffin

by Jon Thibault, photos by Rick Hustead
Black Belt Buyer's Guide 2007

Forrest Griffin is a force to be reckoned with. Hailing from Athens, Georgia, this 6-foot-3-inch, 205-pound light-heavyweight fighter has fought the likes of Elvis Sinosic, Jeremy Horn, Tito Ortiz and Dan Severn and currently sports a professional record of 13 wins, three losses and no draws. Griffin was a member of Chuck Liddell's team on Spike TV's The Ultimate Fighter, emerging victorious over Stephan Bonnar in the season finale to land himself a contract with the Ultimate Fighting Championship.

Q: Can you briefly describe your training regimen?
A: I work, box and wrestle. I've heard good things about *jiu-jitsu*. Right now my hand's a little messed up, so I've been concentrating on my wrestling.

Q: In your fight with Tito Ortiz at the UFC 59: Reality Check, your takedown defense was excellent. In general, are fighters realizing the importance of good takedown defense, or is it still a neglected part of their training?
A: I think everybody knows that you have to use offensive and defensive wrestling, and that's something I've been trying to push and really learn. To tell you the truth, I always thought submissions were fun—a great way to finish a fight. I always loved punching people, so both things were my favorites and I worked on them both.

Q: Staying in the guard rather than passing seems to be the trend right now; a lot of fighters just stay in there and pound away. Which approach do you think is more effective?
A: I try to pass. You've got all the options there, so use the strikes to make the guy open his guard, and then when he goes to open guard, butterfly guard, feet on the hips, whatever. It's a lot of energy for both guys, and that's when you've got to work the pass. Sometimes, late in the fight, you don't want to expend all that energy trying to get around the guy. If you get there, it's worth it, but a lot of times when you go for the pass, it gives the guy the opportunity to stand.

Q: *The Ultimate Fighter* on Spike TV introduced you to millions of viewers. What was it like to become a celebrity so quickly?
A: I just try to ignore it a little. It makes me a little uncomfortable, so I don't worry about it.

Q: Is there a title shot on the horizon?

A: We'll see. I'm not worried about it. I'm not sure that I'm ready, but I plan on being ready.

Griffin's most recent bout at the UFC 62: Liddell vs. Sobral paired him once again with *The Ultimate Fighter* opponent Stephan Bonnar. He won by unanimous decision—*again*.

DAN HENDERSON

Dan Henderson:
2007 MMA Fighter of the Year

by Edward Pollard, photos by Rick Hustead
Black Belt December 2007

Before many of today's mixed-martial arts fans had even discovered the sport, an American wrestler named Dan Henderson was pulverizing opponent after opponent in the cavernous arenas of Japan's biggest MMA promotions: Rings and the PRIDE Fighting Championships. The 6-foot-tall, 180-plus-pound Californian has successfully represented his nation in the Far East since 1999,

garnering a record of 22 wins and five losses. His first two events outside Japan—the Brazil Open '97 and the Ultimate Fighting Championship 17 in 1998—saw him fight twice in each one and win all four encounters. And he hasn't slowed down since.

Born in 1970 and introduced to wrestling at age 5, Henderson grappled in high school and placed twice in California state competitions. He wrestled at Arizona State University and entered the 1993 NCAA Championships. He also represented the United States in Greco-Roman wrestling at the Olympics in 1992 and 1996.

Henderson is a versatile athlete who relies on his Greco-Roman ability and boxing skills to weather the uncertainties of MMA. He has heavy hands that can deliver a knockout when the situation requires it. He's gone the distance 14 times and lost only three of those. In all those bouts, he's never been KO'd. That record speaks volumes about his heart and endurance, two attributes required for success in today's highly competitive field.

Henderson's list of vanquished opponents includes Antonio Rodrigo Nogueira, Murilo Bustamante, Renzo Gracie and Kazuo Misaki. In February 2007, he remedied a December 2000 decision loss to Wanderlei Silva in spectacular fashion at PRIDE 33, knocking the "Axe-Murderer" flat on his back and out cold.

As a member of Oregon's Team Quest, he shares training time and strategies with veterans like Randy Couture, Matt Lindland and Thierry Sokoudjou. He owns his own gym in Murrieta, California, which serves as the Southern Californian branch of Team Quest. At the time of this writing, he holds championship

belts in two weight classes, a feat unmatched by any other MMA athlete.

Throughout his career, Henderson has been impressively consistent. He's a feared opponent with a reputation for possessing enough explosive power to knock out anyone. Not immune to the call of the entertainment world, he recently made a brief appearance on *King of Queens*. Afterward, fans of the fighter and the sitcom noted that his role, which mentioned his missing front teeth, demonstrated something rare in the fight world: the ability to laugh at oneself.

Q & A With Dan Henderson

The pride of PRIDE: The techniques, tactics and training of welterweight champion Dan Henderson.

by Lito Angeles
Black Belt August 2006

Q: In the mixed martial arts, cardio is obviously important. Are your workouts more focused on long-distance training or sprint training?
A: I mix it up. I probably need to do a little more cross-training to up my cardio. I don't run [a lot] because of my back. I do sprints, go mountain-biking and stuff like that. I also do box-hops [plyometrics].

Q: Do you follow a set regimen for the plyometrics?
A: It varies. I usually go for a minute on and 30 seconds off. I do one exercise about eight to 10 times, then another exercise eight to 10 times. Then I do some sprints, sometimes with a bungee, for whatever length the mat is—usually 75 feet.

Q: Do you also use focus pads in your cardio training?
A: Yes. When I do those workouts, I do at least three-minute rounds, sometimes five-minute rounds.

Q: Do you have a set routine, or do you do whatever you decide on that particular day?
A: It's whatever I want to work on that day. If I want to work on combinations or something, I do them a little more. Then I might hit the bag for a couple of rounds, the focus mitts for three or four rounds, and the bag for three or four rounds.

Q: Are your workouts more power- or speed-oriented? When you hit the bag, are you just trying to blast through it, or do you do rapid-fire punches?
A: I try to speed my punches up as much as I can, but most of the time I try to go hard, as well. The difficult thing is to throw really hard and not telegraph the punch.

Q: With strength and weight training, are you a believer in low repetitions with high weight or a lot of reps with moderate weight?
A: High reps with low weight. In some workouts, I do 20 to 30 reps in my low-rep workout. Right now, I'm doing one set of 100 reps for 13 to 14 exercises. I go through it as fast as I can.

Q: Is it a circuit?
A: It's a circuit with machine weights. I get the weight to where I can do 60 to 70 reps nonstop. Then if I

have to stop, I stop for 10 seconds and finish it. It helps with muscle endurance, and it makes me stronger. don't think it would do me a lot of good to max out after three to five reps. I want to make sure my muscles are still there after 19 minutes [of fighting].

Q: Do other mixed martial artists train like that?
A: I don't know how other fighters train, but I'm sure that some of them do. I'm not saying my way is right or wrong; it works for me.

Q: What about flexibility? Do you spend a lot of time stretching?
A: I haven't really done much stretching in the past 15 years. I try to do a little bit, but I'm probably the least flexible guy. I can't touch my toes.

Q: Has that hurt your performance or caused you any injuries?
A: No. I adapt to how my body is.

Q: How do you break up your training, from stand-up to the clinch to the ground? Do you separate the phases or incorporate them all in one workout?
A: We separate them a little bit and bring them together. One or two days a week, we spar—mostly stand-up but we allow takedowns and fighting on the ground with the big gloves on. We don't break when we get in a clinch. On other days, we put on MMA gloves and start on our feet, but we're not standing there sparring We don't spend much time open; we give ourselves 10 seconds to get in a clinch. We throw light strikes and hit each other. On other days, we'll do the same thing in MMA gloves but starting on the ground. But like most training to be on our feet.

Q: How many times a week do you actually fight in the ring?
A: We spar on the lighter days at 70 to 80 percent. At least one day a week, we spar at 100 percent.

Q: With MMA gloves?
A: No. You can't spar 100 percent with MMA gloves.

Q: There's an old saying: The way you train is the way you fight. If you pull your punches in training, do you also find yourself pulling them in fights?
A: I don't have that problem. I punch hard out there. In training with the big gloves, we go 100 percent with takedowns and everything else. With grappling and wrestling, we go 100 percent. It's only the actual striking with MMA gloves that's not as hard.

Q: With 16-ounce gloves, is it difficult to get a good grip for grappling techniques?
A: It's harder to take a guy down and harder to lock your hands. [During that kind of training,] I usually stay on the ground for 20 or 30 seconds, then stand back up.

Q: How many days a week do you go 100 percent?
A: One day a week, sometimes two. If you go hard all the time, people will get hurt. When I say 100 percent I'm not trying to knock the guy out, but sometimes it happens. Body shots are 100 percent; leg shots are 90 to 100 percent. But when I know it's a clean shot, I'm not going to follow through as hard.

Q: You used to be a wrestler, but it seems like you're mainly a striker now and that you use your wrestling to keep from going to the ground or to get back up if you're on the mat so you can ground-and-pound.
A: Yeah, that's my best chance to finish the fight. I'm pretty good on submissions, as well. I guess I just haven't given myself a chance to try to submit guys in fights. It's fun for me to pound on somebody, and that's what promoters and fans like to see.

Q: What do you think of the two opposing philosophies: More is better, and less is best?
A: It's always good to change things up a little bit; you don't want to do the same thing because people will watch your fights and know what you're going to do. And you're not progressing as much as a fighter. But I would rather know a couple of things really well than know a whole bunch of things that I couldn't do on everybody. But you have to know [a variety of techniques] to stop submissions. Plus, it's fun learning all that stuff.

Q: Anyone who studies MMA matches can see what works: the cross-body armbar from the mount, the triangle, the heel hook, the kneebar, the *kimura*. Do you tend to focus on common denominators like those techniques?
A: Yeah. That's pretty much my philosophy. When I teach seminars, it's the stuff I know will work.

Q: Which stand-up techniques are effective for you?
A: The overhand right works well, but it has to have good timing. It's not something that you can just walk out and land on somebody. And I've been working on my body shots and left-hand jabs and hooks.

Q: What got you interested in body shots?
A: Everyone was saying how well they work, and I thought I'd try them.

Q: What about right hooks to the body?
A: I do them, just not as much as left hooks. I typically throw my right to the head and come back with a left to the body.

Q: Uppercuts?
A: They're a big part of my boxing, more so in the clinch. I don't do a lot of uppercuts from out in the open.

Q: How about elbows?
A: In PRIDE, we're allowed to throw elbows, just not to the head. We can elbow the body all we want. I do a lot; most are on the ground. They're a useful tool and can get your opponent to move.

Q: Do you relegate them to secondary status?
A: They're down on the list. Elbows can cut a guy and stop a fight. They don't really knock a guy out.

Q: Just about everyone in MMA does round kicks, and most fighters do front kicks. Side kicks are not used much. Are any other kicks viable in the ring?
A: Sometimes I do spinning kicks in training, but I don't think I've ever done one in a fight. I got caught with one to the body just yesterday. They definitely work, but they take technique and timing.

Q: Do you think a lead-leg round kick does much damage?

A: It mostly annoys the guy and gets him to react so you can set up your hands. If you're fighting a lefty, you can do a lead-leg round kick to his front leg, and it will take its toll.

Q: Do you ever use front kicks?
A: Not a whole lot, but I do them in practice. The guys I train with use them, and it annoys me. I'm always moving forward, and it's easy for them to put up a leg and push me away. I don't think the front kick is a bad kick. It's useful if you're an offensive fighter and not as useful if you're defensive and trying to kick a guy from a distance.

Q: Are knees the only effective strikes you can use in a clinch?
A: There are a lot of things. It depends on how your opponent is reacting. I do a lot of uppercuts from the clinch and elbows to the body to set him up. Knees are easily stopped in the clinch, but they're definitely useful.

Q: In the ring, only knees to the head seem to do damage. Knees to the body seem less effective.
A: No. Knees to the body work well. It's like a boxer doing body shots—they'll wear a guy down. Knees to the thighs are more of an annoyance to get him to move, maybe to set up a takedown.

I learned a long time ago not to tell someone a technique won't work. A lot of it is the setup—how you get into position for it. That's going to be different for everybody. For example, take the overhand right. The way I get into it might not work for everybody. If you like a move, you'll learn it and get good at it. If you don't like it, you should practice it so you don't get caught in it.

Q: With the clinch, is your strategy to get out of it and begin striking again or to take your opponent down?
A: It depends on how good he is on his feet and how tired I am. A lot of times, I'll stay in the clinch and try to beat him up.

Q: It seems that of the three stages of fighting, the clinch is least developed.
A: A lot of guys get in the clinch and stop. I don't like that. I get in a clinch and fight for a while, then fight out of it. Train how you fight.

Q: Let's talk takedown defense. In your opinion, what's the key to the sprawl?
A: The greatest thing is making sure you know where the guy's head is. You want to maintain control of his head—push it down while you sprawl.

Q: With respect to ground fighting, is anything other than the kimura, armbar, triangle, rear-naked choke, guillotine and heel hook effective?
A: I do a lot of stuff from the half-guard and side control. From the half-guard on top, I have a good choke. It's something I discovered on my own and modified. Most of my other stuff involves getting into a position where I can beat on the guy.

Q: Do you spend much time practicing those staples of grappling?
A: I don't. I do them, but I don't drill them that much. If I drill them, it's more for defense.

Q: It seems like the main styles seen in MMA are boxing, *muay Thai*, wrestling, Brazilian *jiu-jitsu* and judo. Would you say they're the arts aspiring fighters should focus on?
A: The biggest components of MMA are wrestling, kickboxing and jiu-jitsu. Judo is a kind of wrestling, and

kickboxing encompasses boxing. I think MMA is the sum of those three things, and in those three things there's so much to learn that you don't need to go outside them too much.

Q: Which art would you advise people to study first?
A: Nowadays, most up-and-coming fighters are from an MMA background. I think that's the best base to have. Most trainers aren't real good at wrestling. They don't know takedowns well because they don't have a wrestling background. If everyone had to fight with a *gi*, I would say it's most beneficial to study Brazilian jiu-jitsu, as well, but that's not the case. Wrestling without a gi is grabbing the body. Wrestling is definitely the [second] best base to have. If you were to learn one of those things growing up, I would suggest wrestling and then transitioning to the other stuff.

Q: What portion of your MMA repertoire would you teach a student interested in self-defense?
A: I'd teach methods for controlling the guy rather than punching: getting into a clinch and taking him down, or getting behind him and controlling him. Most people aren't really good at controlling and don't know how to stop someone from controlling them. And I'd teach ways to not get hit. And maybe to kick him in the groin.

MATT HUGHES

Photo by Fernando Escovar

Matt Hughes on Training, Fighting and Winning

by Christian George
Black Belt February 2008

What do you get when you step inside the octagon with a 170-pound, nine-time Ultimate Fighting Championship welterweight titleholder? A whole lot of pain. Just ask any of Matt Hughes' opponents. With victories over Carlos Newton, Royce Gracie, Frank Trigg, B.J. Penn and others, Hughes, who was *Black Belt's* 2006 NHB Fighter of the Year, has achieved an astounding 43-5 record. In this exclusive interview, the champ talks about the roles that fighting, faith and family have played in his rise to the top.

Q: Did you ever see yourself rising to such prominence in mixed martial arts?
A: Back when I started this sport, I was just doing it as a hobby. I never thought I'd be on TV or make enough money to support a family. I just did what I wanted to do.

Q: In MMA, which style is most important?
A: That's a tough question. You've got to be well-rounded. Wrestling plays such a huge role because you can control where the fight is going to be. Wrestling is definitely up there.

Q: How do you train during the two days leading up to a fight?
A: I work out hard all the way up until weigh-in. I just enjoy it. The day before weigh-in, I only have two practices, about an hour and a half each. I've got my buddies there, [and] we have a good time just doing what we need to be doing.

Q: Do you follow a strict diet?
A: I eat healthy. You don't need a bunch of saturated fat or processed sugar. I like honey. It's not as bad for you as processed sugar. I'll have a sweet potato and put honey on it.

Q: What foods do you stay away from?
A: I'm not a big fast-food guy. You won't see me going to McDonald's or Hardee's—I don't like it. I do eat [at] Subway. If you need something quick, go to Subway.

Q: What's the first thing that goes through your mind when you step into the octagon?
A: I try to focus on my opponent and figure out what I'm going to do. Is my opponent a stand-up artist? Then I use my wrestling offensively, pick him up, put him on the ground and beat him up. Is he a good submission artist? Then I use my wrestling defensively, keep him on his feet and try to win the fight there.

Q: What's the most important factor in executing an effective ground-and-pound game?
A: Learning to strike on the ground is hard to do. You have to work on it.

Q: What other strategies do you keep in mind when you're fighting?
A: Well, I don't bob my head a lot—like a boxer does. I think that you [should] move your feet to get out of the way. A boxer doesn't have to worry about knees and kicks like we do.

Q: Does your family get nervous watching you in the octagon?
A: My wife gets extremely nervous. Some of my family won't even go and watch because there's so much pressure. My grandmother just sits behind a TV and prays.

Q: What advice do you have for martial artists who want to get into MMA?
A: Go out with the mentality of, "I'm not going to

Matt Hughes at *Black Belt's*
Hall of Fame Dinner 2006.
Photo by Robert W. Young

go out there to hurt somebody; I'm going out there to win." That's my mentality. There have been fights when I didn't have to throw a single punch to win. For someone just getting started in the sport, take small steps. Be as well-rounded as you can. Work on your wrestling, striking and submissions.

Q: How should an inexperienced fighter begin competing?

A: Start in the amateurs. Start somewhere low [so] you can get some experience. Don't take fights you can't win. Some people say: "You know, it will be good for me to take this fight even if I lose. I might even last eight to 10 minutes." I disagree.

Q: Speaking of losing, what would you have done differently in the UFC 65 match in which you lost the belt to Georges St. Pierre?

A: I would have spent more time trying to take him down and not stood up so much.

Q: Are you a Bruce Lee fan?

A: Yeah. He was way before his time. Shoot, if he were alive today with the Internet and the way we travel, he would have been so much more popular.

Q: How do you think Lee would have measured up in the octagon?

A: In his weight class, he would have done great!

Q: These days, so many people train in MMA using many styles and fighting methods. What one thing unites them all?

A: Competition. We're all fierce competitors. If there's anything we all share, it's competition one-on-one.

Q: Is that why you fight?

A: Yes. When I give up fighting, it will be because I don't want to compete anymore.

Matt Hughes at *Black Belt's* Hall of Fame Dinner 2006. Photo by Edward Pollard

A MAN OF FAITH

Anyone who's watched the current season of *The Ultimate Fighter*, in which Matt Hughes is coaching one team and his archrival, Matt Serra, is coaching the other, knows that Hughes is a deeply religious man. In his eyes, training spiritually as well as physically offers plenty of payoffs.

"The big benefit is that I take a lot of pressure off my shoulders because I always ask that God's will be done," Hughes says. "It's up to him. If it's God's will that I lose, I'm fine with that. I don't worry about that."

Hughes became a Christian three and a half years ago when he traveled to Guadalupe, Mexico. "I didn't go there to find God, just to work," he says. "There's an orphanage and a school down there, and we were doing construction work. Every night, we had Bible studies, and I had a lot of my questions answered. I was doing a devotional, bowed my head right then and there, and found the Lord. It's one of those things where people ask me, 'How do you know if you're a Christian and how can I tell people about God?' And I say, 'That's very easy. The day, the moment, I became a Christian, I felt it throughout my entire body. I know there's a God out there because as soon as I became a Christian, it was one of the greatest sensations and also a relief.

"My relationship with God is like any relationship: It's a roller-coaster ride. There are ups and downs. It's similar to having a relationship with your kids, wife, brothers and sisters. It's great to feel the presence of Jesus."

—C.G.

Q: What do you enjoy doing the most when you're not fighting?
A: I like being around the house with my 14-month-old daughter, Hannah, and my wife.

Q: What would you tell your son, Joey, if he wanted to be an ultimate fighter?
A: I would discourage it. It's not an easy road. My body is pretty beat up. It's done great things for me and my family—there's always going to be food on the table now—and it's given me some financial freedom. But as a dad, I don't want to see my son go out there and get hit.

Q: Tell me about your book, *Made in America*.
A: It's my biography. It's also about what goes on behind the scenes in the UFC. It's going to be a good book. I wanted the book to be titled *Fighting Solves Everything* because if you want something, you have to fight for it. Whether it's a relationship or a family, it doesn't matter. Now it doesn't have to be a fistfight, but if I want a job, I'm not going to just call once and give up on it. If I want a job,

I'm going to call those people every day. But the publisher thought that *Made in America* would be a better title.

Q: What's next for you and the UFC?
A: The UFC has grown so much lately [that] I don't know. Who knows what will be next? For me, December 29, 2007, is when I fight Matt Serra.

Q: You are 33 years old. Is your body starting to shut down, or are you still at the top of your game?
A: I'm in the best shape of my life.

Q: What do you want to accomplish in the near future?
A: Well, I can't say that I'm really wanting any big things. I don't want any more world titles. If there's one thing I try to do in this world, it's be a good role model. And I want to continue to be a good husband and a good competitor.

QUINTON JACKSON

Q & A With Quinton Jackson

by Lito Angeles and Edward Pollard,
photos by Rick Hustead
Black Belt May 2008

Q: First, I want to commend you on your comeback. You suffered two devastating losses against Wanderlei Silva. How did you get over them?

A: I looked up to Chuck Liddell after he lost to me in Japan. He came back to the UFC and did his thing and became a champion, and he kept the title for a while. I thought, If Chuck can do it, I can do it, too. Losing a fight is like losing a race. If you're a race-car driver, just because you lost a race doesn't make you a bad driver. I wasn't a bad fighter. I'm not going to make excuses, but I know that if I'm at my best, if I have the right tools and if I'm 100 percent or close to 100 percent, I can be the best fighter in the world. I have proved it, and I'm going to keep on proving it.

Q: Did you use any special technique like visualization or positive thinking?
A: There was nothing because I know why I lost. Some people lose and don't know why, then they have problems and don't correct them. I correct the problems I have.

Q: Is that why you changed your training?
A: That's why I changed my trainers and my training partners. If I'm fighting the best people in the world, I need to have the best sparring partners around. I always had good people to roll *jiu-jitsu* with and wrestle with, but that's really not my game. I'll wrestle when I have to, but you'll never see me try to submit somebody.

Q: You're renowned for your slams and strikes. Does your use of those skills come naturally?
A: When I started wrestling at 17, slamming was just something I knew how to do. I would just pick you up and slam you. I wasn't a technical wrestler. I wrestled one full season in high school, then went to college and wrestled in two or three matches.

Q: It's been said that wrestling is the best base art and that all the other arts are easier to learn. If you were to pick one art as a foundation, would it be wrestling?
A: I would pick wrestling because it's the best form of mixed martial arts. Most champions have been wrestlers or understand wrestling. You have to have that basic knowledge to be successful. Guys who have no knowledge of wrestling can do well, but the ones with a basic knowledge of wrestling do the best.

Q: Is it easier to learn the other components of the fight game?

A: It was easier for me to learn kickboxing. It wasn't easier for me to learn jiu-jitsu, though. In jiu-jitsu, you have to drill over and over, and I hate drilling.

Q: Do you prefer sparring?
A: I love sparring. If something is boring to me, I just can't [do it]. I find a lot of things boring. I have to be entertained; things have to be exciting for me.

Q: When you spar, do you go hard all the time?
A: No. Some people have egos and some don't. I don't have an ego. I get tapped out in my gym a lot. I get taken down. But I don't get mad. When somebody spars with me and says, "Let's go easy, let's go light," I go light until they pick it up. Then it turns into a hard thing.

Q: Should a person who's training for self-defense go hard in training?
A: It's good to go light most of the time so you can get your technique down. But with *muay Thai*, sometimes you can't go too slow or too light because the guy will see your kick coming and check it. You have to find that fine line between the right speed and the right power so your partner doesn't get upset and turn it into a fight. A sparring match can turn into a fight really quick—in about two seconds.

Q: Do you also think that training light is the best way to prepare for a fight?
A: No. You go light sometimes, and some days you go hard with your headgear and mouthpiece. It's as simple as that. In muay Thai, you always go hard on the pads. I don't see why you would ever go light on the pads. If you're out of shape, you go for as long as you can on the pads—until you gas out. But if you're in shape, you go as hard as you can go on the pads every time.

Q: How important is weight training?
A: Everybody's different. Personally, I don't lift weights because I don't have time. I'm naturally

strong, so I don't need it. I do push-ups and sit-ups, and that's about it. I've always been this way. I was always stronger than most kids my age. God just gave me a certain strength, and I can only use it at certain times. It's the weirdest thing. I remember fights when I would pick people up and slam them, but I couldn't do it in training. In fights, it just comes out.

Q: What was it like when you were asked to be a coach on *The Ultimate Fighter*?

A: Well, I've never done much coaching. I just scream at my friends and tell them what to do, but they never listen. (smiling) Everybody reacts differently. Some people react if you scream at them: "Hey, come on, dude!" But with some people, it's better if you just talk calmly: "Hey, you just need to go for the armbar," or "You need to put your feet in his hips and push him away and stand up."

Q: What will your approach be?

A: I'll just try to get to know everybody. I have no idea how *The Ultimate Fighter* is structured, how they do anything. I just know that it's going to be a great experience. I'm going to be like a fish out of water. Of course, I expect to do my best and give 110 percent.

Q: Have you watched any of the past seasons of the show?

A: The first season I watched a couple of shows, but I'm not a big TV guy. If I'm in front of a TV, most of the time it's playing video games. I tried to watch *The Ultimate Fighter* because some of my friends were on, but it came on at 10 at night. When I'm training for a fight, I'm in bed by 10.

Q: How do you think the increased exposure you'll have from the show will affect your life?

A: That's something I'm dealing with. I've got to get used to being more popular. Back when I was fighting in Japan, I was more popular, but I could come home and just be a normal guy. In all honesty, I still wish I could be that guy. I wish I could go to the fights and enjoy the fans and get to know them and hang out with them and take pictures with them and then come home and just be myself and hang out with my kids and do whatever I do with my friends—just be myself.

You see, I'm not fighting to be popular or famous. I'm fighting to make money and save money for my kids so they can have it better than I had it growing up.

I love the fans. I don't think anybody loves the fans more than me. But I'm a human being. I have bad days, but most of the time, I'm in a good mood. I'm just afraid of new popularity. It's hard to believe that people want my autograph because I still think of myself as an everyday guy.

RAMPAGE JACKSON CAREER HIGHLIGHTS

2001 PRIDE 17: Surprise KO of Yuki Ishikawa

2002 K-1: KOs Cyril Abidi in kickboxing debut. Defeats Abidi again by decision later that year, then quits kickboxing

2003 PRIDE—Final Conflict: Defeats Chuck Liddell when the "Iceman's" corner stops the fight

2006 WFA—King of the Streets: Defeats Olympic silver-medalist Matt Lindland

2007 UFC 71: Defeats Chuck Liddell again to become the UFC light-heavyweight champion

2007 UFC 75: Defeats PRIDE middleweight champion Dan Henderson, unifying the UFC and PRIDE titles

—Compiled by Jason William McNeil

Q: You've certainly got everyday ears. They haven't been banged up yet. How do you manage that?

A: I don't know. Some people get it the first month they do grappling and jiu-jitsu, but my ears haven't got there yet.

Q: Do you drain them when they swell?

A: I've never had to. When I feel like my ear gets touched or rubbed the wrong way, I stop and grab it. [My opponent is] seriously going for the takedown, and I just grab my ear and rub it. If he tries to submit me or get me in a triangle choke, I'm rubbing my ear. Then I get out [of the hold] and move on him. I want to keep my ears the way God made them.

Q: How about your nose? Have you had your nose broken?

A: I've had my nose broken; it's not the worst thing. When I retire from fighting, I want to get it fixed—or not. I don't care. It's part of who I am as a fighter. It's character, you know? I try to be a realist, to be myself and to stay humble. The crazy thing is that the fighters on a reality show get famous overnight.

Everybody knows their name and face, and then their friends will change—even if they don't change. Some people get busy, and their friends want to hang out with them. They say, "Oh, let's do this," and I'm like, "No, I've got to train for my next fight." And then they think I've changed. That's what we go through.

And I'm not complaining. It's just one of the new things that come with the UFC. It's crazy. In my first fight, I got the UFC jitters. I heard about them, but I didn't think I was going to get them.

Q: What was that like?

A: It's like having your first fight again—and I've fought in front of 70,000 people in Japan. I learned how to deal with it. I'm smart enough to figure things out pretty quick. When I'm training, if I'm doing jiu-jitsu with somebody and they flatten me out with a certain move, that guy will be lucky if he can get me twice with the same move. I adapt. I just have to adapt to this stardom.

Q: If someone were to ask you which arts and skills you'd recommend for self-defense, what would you say?

A: Train in muay Thai kickboxing. Muay Thai is the best form of self-defense because you can use all your tools: elbows, knees, kicks and punches. If a person is giving you problems on the street, most of the time that person won't know any martial arts, so you could probably take on more than one person at a time with muay Thai.

Q: How about Brazilian jiu-jitsu and wrestling?

A: They should be secondary because most fights go to the ground, but when you're on the street, you try not to go to the ground. You want to strike as many people as you can. I've been jumped a lot, and I never wanted to go to the ground because then you have to deal with stomping and all the good stuff. You're very vulnerable. Jiu-jitsu isn't going to help you if there are two or more people.

Q: Were you able to avoid going to the ground in your street fights?

A: No. I got stomped. I went to the ground a lot before I started wrestling. I got kicked in the [groin] and stomped in the head. If I'd known muay Thai, I could have gotten away with stand-up.

Q: What are your top techniques for self-defense?

A: The techniques you should know involve using your knees and elbows because those are the hardest parts of your body. The right cross is great. The jab—why would you try to use the jab? A jab is used to set stuff up, but in self-defense you want stuff that will knock your opponent out. If you kick most people in the leg, they'll leave you alone. One of my friends messes with me all the time because I'm a fighter. When he won't leave me alone, I kick him in the leg. If you give somebody a good kick to the leg, the muscle will go into shock if his body isn't used to it. So I'd recommend a muay Thai kick to the outside thigh.

FALLEN ANGEL

by Jason William McNeil
BOOK EXCLUSIVE

Though Quinton Jackson did put in a season as a coach on Spike TV's *The Ultimate Fighter* Season 7, his training tenure is remembered more for his outbursts of temper than the skill of his stable. Only two of his fighters advanced to the final round, compared to six finalists from show rivals Team Griffin (coached by Forrest Griffin.) In the season finale, Griffin's fighter, Amir Sadollah, took out Jackson's top fighter, C.B. Dollaway, with an armbar in the match's first round.

Adding insult to injury, Jackson lost the light-heavyweight title to Griffin (via split decision) at the UFC 86. Full of righteous indignation, Jackson's coach-manager-mentor Juanito Ibarra announced that he planned to protest the decision with the Nevada State Athletic Commission. However, he later decided against filing said protest after discussing the matter with the commission.

Shortly thereafter, Jackson fired Ibarra.

So, with his spiritual and professional lives seemingly separated, and with talks of a Jackson/Griffin rematch building buzz, one would think it'd be back to business for "Rampage," right?

Again, that's what one might expect. …

On July 15, 2008, Jackson was arrested and booked on suspicion of felony reckless driving as well as a felony hit-and-run after allegedly striking several vehicles, leading police on a chase, and driving on the wrong side of the street and on sidewalks. Even after blowing a tire, he allegedly continued on the rim, showering sparks across the road.

One can't help but wonder how Jackson expected to escape because his alleged escape vehicle was a modified and lifted Ford F-350 truck with his picture painted on the side.

Three days later, Ultimate Fighting Championship President Dana White told Yahoo Sports that Jackson had been taken to a mental institution on July 16 for a "72-hour observation," adding that the stay had been extended.

"I think it's going to be a while before we get him back," White said. He added that Jackson had been depressed over his loss to Griffin and, while no drugs were found in his system at the time, Jackson "did not sleep for four days and was not eating, only drinking water and energy drinks."

If that turns out to be the end of Jackson's powerful and always-unpredictable presence in the world of mixed martial arts, then it'll be an ending even the best guessers could never have predicted. However, for those who've watched the rise and fall—and rise and fall and fall further—of Quinton Jackson, the only constant is that he constantly defies expectations.

Have we seen the last of Jackson? Probably not? How and when will he make his return? There's no way to tell.

Count on this, though: If and when Jackson returns, it'll be in a way nobody ever, ever expected.

Editor's note: Quinton Jackson avenged his losses to Wanderlei Silva by knocking him out at the UFC 92. He also beat Keith Jardine at the UFC 96 in March 2009.

CUNG LE

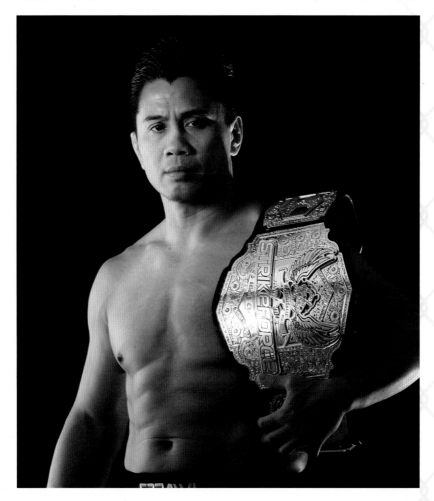

Train to Be a Mixed-Martial Arts Champion!

Exclusive interview with Strikeforce middleweight titleholder Cung Le.

by Edward Pollard, photos by Rick Hustead
Black Belt December 2008

Cung Le, the *Black Belt* Hall of Fame member who transformed himself from *sanshou* champion to MMA fighter to the man who vanquished Frank Shamrock on March 29, 2008, in a Strikeforce/EliteXC event, tells you what you need to do to climb to the top.

Q: You made your name in sanshou before migrating to the mixed martial arts. How long have you been doing MMA?
A: Since 2005. I had my first fight in 2006, and two years later, I beat Frank Shamrock for the Strikeforce middleweight title.

Q: What changes were required for you to move to MMA?
A: I had to go from three-round fights to five-round fights. I had to increase my cardio and strength training, my mitt work, my ground work and my grappling game.

Q: One of the most important components of martial arts training is stretching. You were known for your high kicks when you competed in sanshou, so you evidently think stretching is important. How do you develop your flexibility for MMA?

A: I start with deep lunges and follow with basic stretches from the neck down. Then I do my regular stretching routine, which is walking up and down the mat doing lunges, and on each step, I swing one leg straight up. Then I do it again and swing each leg from the inside out like a circle kick. After that, I warm up with light shadowboxing to get my blood and heart rate up. I do that before my main workout, which usually involves lifting weights, doing cardio exercises and grappling.

Q: What dangers crop up when a fighter tries to use high kicks in an MMA match?

A: It takes time to develop your high kicks. In training, you have to limit yourself so you don't overstretch your muscles or tear something when you swing your leg with full power. You have to realize, too, that not everyone is flexible enough to be able to kick high in competition.

When you get to the advanced level, you should know your body well, but not everyone does. If you want to be an MMA champ, you have to be prepared to do a lot more training than your average nine-to-fiver who works out in the gym down the street.

Q: You mentioned overstretching. I've heard from other competitors that too much stretching before a workout or fight can make you more prone to injury.

A: I don't believe that. I like to stretch before and after. Stretching is actually part of my training. Of course, there's only so much pain your body can take, and you never want to [push] any exercise to where there's a lot of pain. Never stretch so much that you feel intense pain because you might hurt something. Get familiar with your limits.

Q: For success in MMA, do you think it's important to be flexible enough to do the splits?

A: Whether you're a mixed martial artist or a practitioner of any individual martial art, the more flexible you are, the better. I still can't do a complete split—I'm close, though, and I'm getting better.

Q: Which is more important in your training, cardio or strength?

A: I have to work both, but I change my workout a lot. If I start with strength training for a couple of weeks and my body gets used to it, I switch places and start with cardio exercises.

Q: What's your reasoning?

A: The human body quickly gets used to routines, so you have to confuse your muscles to get faster results. That means changing your workout and confusing your muscles instead of doing a regular routine day in and day out. The body gets [the message] that you're doing something different when you mix things up.

Q: What's the benefit of confusing your muscles?

A: When you hit a plateau, you can lose track of your peak. It stalls your progress, but it lets you know that you need a change. You have to make your body adapt to new situations because if you get used to one thing, you'll only be in shape for doing that. What happens when you're faced with your opponent's routine? Introducing something new to your body is the way to reach the next level.

Q: What has worked for you in cardio training?

A: I do a lot of sprints and spend a lot of time on elliptical and high-altitude machines. High-altitude machines simulate training at 5,000 feet or even 12,000 feet—you wear a mask that limits your oxygen intake. A typical session lasts from 30 to 35 minutes, and I do different variations, the same as I do to my muscles.

Q: How do you monitor your progress?

A: I take notes and track my output in strides per minute.

Q: How do you measure your cardio development?

A: It depends on how hard I push it. In my cardio session, I can push to 100 percent, but I can't do that all the time. The benefit of fighting in the ring or cage is that you know the maximum time you'll be fighting. If it's three rounds, you train for four rounds. I like to train for an extra round and then gauge my progress by the way my body reacts.

Q: What are your strength routines like?
A: I do super sets and giant sets. In a superset, you change machines once. In a giant set, you use multiple machines. An example of a giant set is, you do bench presses, flyes and cables without any rest from one machine to another. I do a lot of *muay Thai* neck wrestling. I train my whole body and always use different variations.

Q: How do you develop the fighting techniques you need in MMA?
A: I try to balance punching, kicking, knee strikes and shadowboxing. Next, I go to mitt training, which focuses on the upper body, and kicking the high pad. Finally, I put it all together and do punching and kicking with the high pad.

During this phase of training, you have to concentrate on proper technique. Also important is doing punching and kicking combinations, including transitions between them. You should also work on the clinch and close-up knee strikes, single- and double-leg takedowns, and throwing punches on the way out and on the way in.

Q: When it comes to techniques, you're able to draw from a variety of styles because you've been in the martial arts for so long. Which ones do you find most useful for MMA?
A: I did wrestling—freestyle, Greco-Roman and collegiate style. Then I took up *taekwondo,* which helped me with my kicking, and kung fu, which is where I got my scissor kick. Now I'm doing a lot of *jiu-jitsu* and submission wrestling.

Q: Do you do any boxing?
A: Boxing is part of my stand-up training. That includes kickboxing and muay Thai, plus a lot of pad work and sparring.

Q: Which aspect of the fight game has given you the most trouble?

A: Definitely the ground—particularly jiu-jitsu. It's fun to learn, but it takes a lot of time and puts a lot of wear and tear on your body, especially the joints.

Q: You're 36. Are you finding that certain aspects of your martial arts training are getting more difficult as you age?

A: Not really. It's just a matter of learning how to listen to your body.

Q: Let's talk about nutrition. Do you ever go to extremes such as following a vegetarian diet?

A: No, I need meat in my diet. My diet is 70-percent organic. As far as supplements go, I use several kinds of powdered wheatgrass or Vitamineral Green, amino acids and the omegas (3 and 6). Most of the time when I'm training, I go for chicken or beef broth, organic pasta, and free-range chicken or organic red meat.

Q: What's the latest you'll eat before a workout?

A: I can eat an hour before training, and I'm fine.

Q: With this layer of increased intensity in your training, do you enjoy the martial arts as much as you did before?

A: I love to train; you don't get into this unless you do. When you go into MMA, it becomes your job and your focus. If you need to do something extra, you do it. You don't pop in for an hour and then get out.

Q: Do you have any advice for martial artists who have day jobs but still want to break into MMA?

A: You have to be serious about it. It can be life changing in good and bad ways. If you're a weekend MMA fighter, you'd better have a good promoter who puts on a solid card. The right exposure can mean the difference between getting noticed and just being another guy. Your brain and body are on the line, so you should always have a professional attitude when you train. Find a good trainer and work with good partners. Then make sure you study your opponent so you don't get thrown to the wolves.

THE CHINESE CONNECTION

By Dr. Mark Cheng
Black Belt December 2008

Ush! It's the last sound you hear before the glove crashes into your face, the spinning back kick knocks the air out of your lungs or your head collides with the mat after the suplex. For decades, people have criticized kung fu stylists for being weak on fighting experience, but Cung Le has stood tall to prove them wrong time and again in the ring and in the cage.

While many of his peers were content to do forms and continuous light sparring, Le found his calling in *sanshou*, China's brand of full-contact fighting. With rules that allow the fullest expression of combat training—which, in Le's case, includes wrestling, *taekwondo* and Vietnamese kung fu—sanshou's combination of kickboxing with throws and takedowns fit him like a glove.

Once he mastered the basics, Le set about conquering the tournament scene. He won his first national sanshou title in Orlando, Florida, in 1994. In 1995 he represented the United States at the International Wushu Federation sanshou tournament and brought home the bronze. He's the only American athlete to medal three times in international sanshou competition.

Not one to rest on his laurels, Le was driven to further sharpen his fighting skills. While critics complain that the techniques a martial artist uses in a demonstration are flashier than those used in a real fight, Le proved that hard training can make even the most incredible moves look easy. From his flying leg-scissor takedowns to his suplex throws to his jump spinning kicks, he brought real excitement back to even the most jaded fight fans.

SANSHOU

By Jason William McNeil
BOOK EXCLUSIVE

Sanshou, the Chinese version of kickboxing, was first developed in its modern form in 1979 by the Chinese Wushu Institute. It was officially sanctioned in 1990.

While the rules of sanshou competition may vary slightly from promotion to promotion and event to event, the sport differentiates itself from other styles of kickboxing by following a fairly consistent core set of guidelines.

➜ Competitors wear boxing gloves.

➜ One-point, two-point and three-point scores are awarded for successfully delivered techniques.

➜ Barring a knockout, the fighter who has won the most rounds is declared the winner.

➜ Matches are fought either on a *lei tai* (special raised platform) or in a boxing ring with no side ropes or ring posts.

➜ Legal attacks include punches, kicks, sweeps and throws.

➜ Elbow strikes are not allowed.

➜ Knee strikes are sometimes allowed, but this must be determined and agreed to by both parties before the match.

➜ In some matches, points are awarded for driving one's opponent off the fighting platform or deducted from the score of the fighter going off the lei tai. This is not universal, however, and some promotions prohibit pushing from the fighting area and even deduct penalty points for each infraction. This is mostly because of safety concerns, but it's also to encourage clean technique over sumo-style pushing, pulling and shoving.

GENE LEBELL

Gene LeBell: The Godfather of Grappling

by Jason William McNeil, photos by Rick Hustead
BOOK EXCLUSIVE

"I first met Bruce Lee on the set of *The Green Hornet*," Gene LeBell explains, taking a breather from twisting an up-and-coming fighter into a particularly nefarious leg pretzel. "When I got there, Benny Dobbins, the stunt director, told me to 'go put Bruce in a head lock or something.' Well, I try to be a good employee, and Benny was the boss, so I went over and picked Bruce up

over my shoulder, like in a fireman's carry. Bruce was making all these crazy noises—like he'd later become famous for—so, as a joke, I ran up and down the length of the set carrying him!

"Bruce said to me, 'When you put me down, I'm going to kill you,' so I ran up and down the set again. He said, 'Put me down!' and I told him, 'I can't put you down, or you'll kill me!' Then I sat

down and talked to my boss and the crew for a few minutes with him on my shoulder. Later, we all had a good laugh about it and shot some really good scenes. We ended up becoming friends and working out together, though I always hated going to his home gym because of the stinky incense he always burned there.

"Bruce loved to learn grappling. He couldn't get enough of it, but he said it would never be popular as entertainment because the fights were over too fast and most of the action was hidden. It wasn't flashy and acrobatic enough for the camera. I wish he could be around now to see how well grappling is doing these days.

"One of the locks Bruce really liked was this one," and the story ends with another student wincing in pain, as LeBell cranks an "illegal" ankle lock.

The man dubbed the "Godfather of Grappling" loves to spin a round, unvarnished tale, but all his stories seem to end the same: with pain. He can crack a rib or a smile with equal ease, and he often does the two together.

Despite having entered his seventh decade, LeBell draws scores of students. Night after night, they show up hoping to gain a little wisdom, a little ring savvy, and a whole heaping helping of fighting skill gleaned from a life spent grappling with whatever the world threw his way. It's not for nothing that the greatest names in mixed martial arts as well as the rough-and-tumble world of professional stuntmen speak LeBell's name with love and respect and have bestowed on him the title "Toughest Man Alive."

THE PINK GI

" The Toughest Man Alive" wears a pink *gi*. Why not? Who's going to tell him he can't? But still—pink? Why? And where did Gene LeBell's sartorial signature come from?

Like many an unexpected pink garment, it all started with a laundry accident.

While competing in a national judo tournament in Japan, LeBell's gi was sent to the laundry, where it was accidentally washed with a pair of red shorts that had somehow mixed in with the load. When the gi was returned the next evening, just before the competition, it was a lovely, if untraditional, shade of pink. Not having a handy backup uniform, LeBell had little choice but to wear the daintily hued judo gi to the competition.

Not incidentally, he won.

The next day, LeBell recalls, the Japanese newspapers reported that the American *daikon* had won the national judo title. "I later found out that daikon is Japanese for 'radish.' Because of the pink gi and my red hair, they thought I looked like a radish and stuck me with that nickname," he says.

Recognizing a good gimmick when he saw it, LeBell embraced the pink gi as his trademark, and the color of rose petals and blushing brides has become forever synonymous with the "Godfather of Grappling."

—JWM

Mixing It Up

To look at LeBell is to look straight into the face of three-quarters of a century of grappling, wrestling, boxing, fighting, jumping off buildings, falling through windows, riding and crashing motorcycles, and any number of other ways a man can make a living laughing in the face of danger. His nose has been broken so many times it's bulbous, his ears are so cauliflowered they make Randy Couture's seem dainty, and his 76-year-old face reads like a road map of a life lived the hard way. But amid the crags, crevasses and scars of a face that resembles a shrunken apple carving, there's something else always stretched across the surface: a smile. He's just as quick with a joke as he is with a head lock, and he has an uncanny knack for dispensing humor, pain and wisdom simultaneously. He's earned his scars and learned a thing or two along the way. And the martial arts elite continue to wear a path to his door, hoping to drink a bit from the man's vast well of knowledge. LeBell's done it all before, pal, and the fun stuff he did twice. The stuff that

GENE LEBELL CAREER HIGHLIGHTS

1954—National AAU heavyweight judo champion and overall judo champion

1955—Repeated as National AAU judo champion (won 17 of 18 matches using only standing throws)

1960—World Wrestling Championships winner (for 12 seconds)

1963—Defeated Milo Savage in a "boxer vs. judo/karate" match, (choked fourth-ranked boxer Savage unconscious in fourth round)

1976—Refereed infamous "boxing vs. wrestling" match between Muhammad Ali and Antonio Inoki

1991—*Black Belt* Hall of Fame—*Black Belt* magazine

1995—Iron Mike Mazurki Award "Cauliflower Alley Club"

2000—Promoted to ninth *dan* in U.S. *jujutsu* and U.S. *taihojutsu* by the U.S. Ju-Jitsu Federation

2005—George Tragos/Lou Thesz Professional Wrestling Hall of Fame

2005—Promoted to ninth dan in traditional Kodokan judo by the U.S. Ju-Jitsu Federation

2007—Judged the UFC 74: Respect (featured Randy Couture vs. Gabriel Gonzaga)

—Compiled by JWM

wasn't so much fun—well, he did that, too, but he made sure he got paid extra for it.

LeBell has been mixing martial arts since before there was a word for it. He's beaten the Japanese at judo and beaten boxers in the ring. He's coached champions, judged the Ultimate Fighting Championship, and was even the World Heavyweight Professional Wrestling champion for all of 12 seconds (more on that later). In the world of grappling and mixed martial arts, the name of Gene LeBell is spoken with both fondness and respect. They call him the "Godfather of Grappling" without a hint of irony.

As if reverence from the world's most ferocious fighters wasn't enough, LeBell also commands the same level of respect and admiration from an entirely different field of professional badasses: the alpha-male world of Hollywood stuntmen. With a career spanning from the early 1960s through last week, tipping the counter at a thousand films and TV shows and still going strong, everybody

who's anybody in the Hollywood stunt game knows and respects LeBell. And they still call him up for work at an age when most grandpas spend their waking hours getting on close terms with an easy chair.

Most MMA fighters not named Gracie can point to the time when they decided to take up the fight game. LeBell, however, was born into it—literally.

His widowed mother, Aileen Eaton, owned and operated the Grand Olympic Auditorium in Los Angeles (which had been built for the 1932 Olympic Games) in the 1940s, where she was a successful and pioneering promoter in the fields of boxing and professional wrestling. Lacking a strong father figure, young LeBell gravitated to the larger-than-life tough men who came and went and worked for his mother at her gym. Legendary fighters passed through the auditorium on a regular basis, including "Gorgeous" George Wagner, Jerry Quarry, Jim Londos, John "The Golden Greek" Tolos, Sugar Ray Robinson, Archie Moore, Sonny Liston, Joe Frazier, Henry

Armstrong, Gene Fullmer, Emile Griffith, Floyd Patterson, Lauro Salas, Ike Williams, Mando Ramos, Danny Lopez, Carlos Palomino, Jimmy Carter, Art Aragon, Sugar Ramos, Carlos Ortiz, Willie Pep, Lou Thesz and many, many more. (Later on, Muhammad Ali and even Andre "The Giant" played the Olympic.) At the early age of 6, an impressionable young LeBell grew up on the mats with a steadily rotating cast of the world's greatest fighters and mixed it up with the legends.

Even among the cavalcade of Golden Age greats who populated LeBell's youth, a couple of "champ encounters" stand out as turning points in his rise to grappling greatness. At age 7, LeBell asked Ed "Strangler" Lewis for instruction, and the 300-pound wrestler literally took young LeBell under his wing. "Ed slapped a head lock on me," LeBell recalls with surprising fondness, "and I felt like the room was spinning for 10 minutes.

"Ed started me out in the world of grappling," he explains, "not wrestling because wrestling has different rules. I loved it because in grappling, you could do just about anything to your opponent. You can hit the guy, do ankle locks, armbars, neck locks, even tweak his nose. And, of course, you can always choke 'em out."

Another memorable encounter came when LeBell found himself in the ring with none other than Sugar Ray Robinson. At the time, LeBell trained in boxing at Main Street Gym in Los Angeles, home to many of the West Coast's boxing champs. Four years later, LeBell happened to be at the gym when Robinson approached and asked whether he felt like sparring. Showing early inklings of the humor in the face of violence that would become his calling card, LeBell says he agreed to spar the welterweight champion and promised not to hurt him. "Of course, after he hit me with about 300 jabs, we called it a day, and I told him to come back tomorrow if he wanted another beating," he recalls.

Around the same time he started boxing at Main Street Gym, a 12-year-old LeBell also began his formal training in judo. Though he was

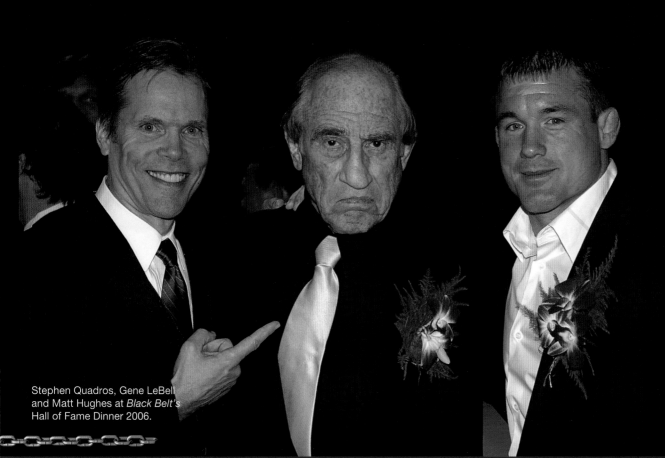

Stephen Quadros, Gene LeBell and Matt Hughes at *Black Belt's* Hall of Fame Dinner 2006.

disqualified from his first judo tournament at age 14 for supposedly performing illegal grappling moves, dropping elbows, and just generally terrorizing opponents, LeBell wasn't deterred from the world of competition. "I don't count disqualifications as losses," LeBell insists. "If you've never been disqualified, you've never been afraid of your opponent."

Thankfully, LeBell continued his climb through the ranks of early American judo competition. His efforts paid off in 1954 when a 21-year-old LeBell pinned John Osako (then considered America's best *judoka*), winning two national judo champion-ships back to back.

Critics at the time dismissed LeBell's champion sweep as a fluke, claiming he had "more luck than skill." The following year, LeBell silenced the critics by repeating his feat, winning 18 matches in two days to take the 1955 Judo National Champion-ships, as well. With characteristic self-effacing humor, LeBell says of his back-to-back national titles: "Even though I only weighed 160 pounds, it wasn't that hard to beat the judo heavyweights. I'd been training with 300-pound wrestlers. At that time, the wrestlers were tougher."

With two national championships and 15

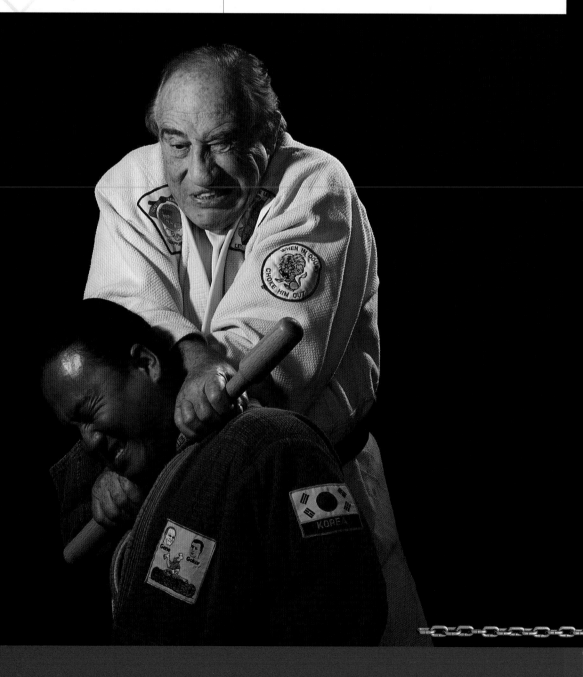

years of hard-core grappling training under his black belt, LeBell set his sights on the Land of the Rising Sun. He traveled to Japan with an Air Force group to train and compete with the world's best judoka, *karateka* and even *aikidoka,* often working out in Tokyo's' Kodokan, the world headquarters of judo.

"At the Kodokan, we'd work what we called 'the slaughter lines,'" LeBell recalls, "where you would just keep fighting guys until you lost." He regularly ran through lines of 20.

It was also in Japan that a laundry accident landed LeBell his trademark pink *gi.*

Despite his national and international tournament successes, LeBell found that the world of amateur athletic competition wasn't paying the bills, so—perhaps recalling the larger-than-life grappling gods who strode like giants through his youth—he decided to try his hand at professional wrestling. His first pro-wrestling match was in 1955, and naturally, it was held at the Grand Olympic Auditorium. After a single match as a "baby face" (good guy), LeBell decided he'd make a better "heel" (wrestling parlance for "bad guy") and set about becoming the nastiest baddie he could be, sometimes even wearing a hood as a character called "The Hangman." He wore the disguise to avoid embarrassing his family, he explains with a laugh.

LeBell's pro-wrestling career peaked in 1960 when he defeated Pat O'Connor in Austin, Texas, to win the World Wrestling Championship belt—for all of 12 seconds. In what he insists was a real accident (draw your own conclusions, fight fans), LeBell became so excited with his newly won title that he swung the championship belt around wildly, accidentally smacking the wrestling commissioner in the face. Enraged, the commissioner disqualified LeBell and stripped him of his title. Ever stoic in the face of adversity, LeBell quips, "At least I got to be the champ for 12 seconds, and I retired on top."

Having scaled and spelunked the heights and depths of the amateur and professional grappling games, LeBell found that he still had bills to pay and not much in the bank to show for his impressive ring record. "I had won over 200 trophies," he says, with a growl, "and if I cashed them all in, they wouldn't make a single house payment." Known as a tough guy who could take a punch and sell a fall, LeBell had begun performing stunts for movies and television since 1955. Eventually, that career gradually grew to eclipse the less-profitable fight game.

"In my fighting career, I won over 2,000 matches in eight years. I beat half a dozen Olympic gold medalists and world champions, and all that winning never made one car payment," LeBell explains. "Now, in the movies, I get beaten up by every wimp in Hollywood, and I've got houses, cars, around three-dozen motorcycles, and I've got a really great life—and that all comes from losing."

It's a Hollywood cliché that off-screen, LeBell has never lost a fight, while on-screen, he's never won a fight. Even though he makes a pretty good living being beaten up by everyone from Jerry Lewis and Eddie Murphy to Ruth Buzzi ("She blindsided me!"), it's in the *dojo,* training the next generation (and the next and the next) of the world's toughest MMA fighters that LeBell is truly at home. He has trained six national judo champions, including U.S. titleholder Gokor Chivichyan, with whom he runs a Los Angeles dojo.

"There were a lot of beautiful judo players in the old Soviet Union, but no one like Gene," Chivichyan says. "I hope I have half his strength when I'm his age."

Ask anyone whose felt themselves on the business end of a LeBell head lock, and they'll tell you in no uncertain terms that the man in pink is an unstoppable force on the mat. Even though he sees himself these days more as a teacher (albeit an internationally renowned one) than a fighter, LeBell still puts on his pink gi and rolls on the mat with students half and even a quarter his age, never letting them forget that, for all his teasing humor and grandfatherly appearance, the "Godfather of Grappling" is still the toughest man alive.

WHEN IN DOUBT, CHOKE 'EM OUT!

" Without question, a choke-out is a fight finisher," the "Godfather of Grappling" declares. Gene LeBell is so well-known for choke-outs that it's something of a rite of passage in his *dojo* to be put out by the master.

What's disturbing is that he seems so good-natured about it. He smiles. He explains what's going on and even jokes as your brain is shutting down from lack of oxygen. No matter how prepared you think you may be, once the choke is on, something primal takes over and you start to twitch and even flail, all to no avail. LeBell's choked out a thousand people, and he'll choke out a thousand more. He's choked out champions. He's choked out movie stars. He's even choked out Superman, so there's nothing special about you, buddy. You're in (relatively) safe hands—experienced hands, at least—but those hands are putting you out. Cold.

"So what I'm doing," you hear him explain as his rear-triangle choke inches tighter around your neck like the slow, murderous advance of a particularly wrinkled python, "is slowing the blood flow to his brain. This is technically a 'strangle,' since we're stopping blood and not just air, which is a choke, but he doesn't really care about that right now."

You can't help it. You want out. You tap a few times, frantically, but the squeezing pressure continues. You're starting to see black spots. You realize, with all certainty, that you're actually going to pass out. You're helpless. This man could kill you if he so desired, and there's nothing you can do to stop him.

"Now I'm stopping the blood flow, and I'm going to count back from 10. Ten, nine, eight ..."

Your ears feel like they're going to pop, and with your last vestige of consciousness, you really, *really* hope you don't piss your pants while you're out.

"... seven, six, five. ..."

Next thing you know, LeBell's squatting over your head, lightly tapping your face to revive you.

My God, you think, how long was I out?

As the world swims back into focus, LeBell sits you up and manipulates several pressure points on your back and shoulders, then leans in and whispers gently in your ear: "So tell me, what did you dream of?"

—JWM

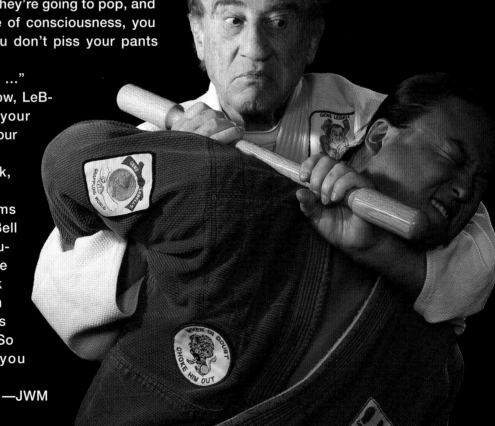

THE ABSOLUTELY (MOSTLY) TRUE STORY OF HOW CHUCK NORRIS STOLE GENE LEBELL'S BLACK BELT

Although Gene LeBell likes to say that belts don't mean much to him, he does like to tell the tale of the one that got away.

"I've always advocated cross-training in martial arts," he explains. "I think that any fighter who doesn't want to learn from anyone of skill is crazy. And it's never a one-way street. I've learned just as much, if not more, from working out with great martial artists like Bruce Lee, Benny 'The Jet' [Urquidez] and Bill Wallace as they ever got from me. However, one thing I can say that Chuck Norris got from me that I never got back was my black belt.

"You see, Chuck's a very humble guy, but that humbleness hides a vicious kleptomaniac. One of the first times I worked out with Chuck was in the gymnasium at Los Angles City College. He came in wearing his *gi*, ready to work out, and I noticed he had on a white belt. Well, I thought to myself, Here's Chuck Norris, a world-renowned black belt, and he's wearing a white belt.

"Now, I understood that Chuck is a very modest man, and he was wearing a white belt as a sign of respect. However, when I teach, I feel that anyone with skill—especially a black belt—can bring something to the class and teach some of his techniques. Again, it's all about the cross-training. Now, if that person were afraid of getting beat up, then he might wear a white belt to throw the instructor off, but I knew that wasn't the case with Chuck. Like I said, he's a very modest person.

"So I said to him, 'Hey, Chuck, you wear a black belt don't you?' and he said, 'I didn't bring a black belt with me.' So I decided to loan him one of my belts, with my name stitched on it; you know, 'Gene LeBell.'

"We worked out and had a good time. Afterward, I'm finished and sitting there waiting for my belt back, and Chuck just left. He took it with him. I knew then and there how much Chuck Norris wanted to be just like me.

"So I go up to Chuck's dear, dear friend, Bob Wall, who was training with us, and said, 'Bob, Chuck took my belt!' and Bob said, 'Well, tough. That's what he does to ugly guys.'

"Next thing I know, Chuck's back in Texas doing this movie called *Sidekicks*, and he's rehearsing with Bob Wall, wearing a karate gi and my black belt. Apparently, a dozen or so kids were watching them work out and one of them noticed that Chuck was wearing my belt. One of the kids asked Bob, 'Why is Mr. Norris wearing a belt with someone else's name on it?' and Bob, the honest upright citizen that he is, told the kids that the only way you get to wear someone else's black belt is to defeat them in a death match.

"So Bob Wall calls me on the phone and tells me, 'Gene, it seems that in Houston, you're now a dead man.' I can't get work in Texas to this day. And to top it all off, Chuck still has my belt. In fact, there's this great picture that gets printed a lot of Chuck Norris and Bob Wall standing back to back. If you look, you can see that Chuck's wearing my black belt with my name on it."

—JWM

AND NOW, THE REALLY REAL STORY BEHIND ONE OF GENE LEBELL'S FAVORITE STORIES

The truth of the matter is that Gene LeBell really did insist that Chuck Norris wear a black belt for their workout at the Los Angeles City College gym and really did give Norris one of his own with "Gene LeBell" embroidered on it.

However, at the end of the day, LeBell told Norris to keep the belt "for next time he came to the *dojo*," and Norris continues to wear it to this day. Norris says he considers it an honor to have been given the belt, embroidered with LeBell's name, and wears it as a sign of respect.

—JWM

CHUCK LIDDELL

Liddell's Leadership Lesson

by Edward Pollard, photos by Rick Hustead
Black Belt March 2005

Q: How do you take an athlete who's had some training but is still fairly inexperienced to a place where he can compete in the octagon?
A: The first thing you've got to do is check where he's at, what he's good at and where his strengths lie. A lot of times, he doesn't even know. He may think his strength is in one thing when actually he's better at something else.

Q: If a guy comes to the gym and says he wants to compete, how do you assess his skill?
A: Usually, I take what he says he knows and check him out on that. This is for guys who come to me and want to fight. I don't ask them to fight. You can't teach someone to want to fight. He has to like fighting.

Q: Let's say someone arrives with grappling skills and proves he knows a few things.
A: If he's got good submission skills or takedowns

and he's a good wrestler, that will be the thing we work on the least. We'll try to keep it sharp because that's the main part of his game, but I don't need to work with him on that too much. I'll probably need to change a few things to make his skills good for submission fighting. The first thing I'd teach him is counter-submissions and how to strike.

It's the same with a striker. The big thing is teaching him counter-wrestling—how to counter submissions so he's not going out there, throwing a couple of punches, getting taken down and getting squashed. That happens a lot with good strikers because they're not comfortable on the ground. They get so afraid to throw punches that their timing is off—they don't land their punches.

Another big thing is seeing what kind of shape he's in. Once we get a guy to the point where he's technically good enough with submission, wrestling and striking skills, I'll put him in a straight kickboxing smoker.

Q: Can you define a "smoker"?
A: Basically, it's slang for glorified sparring. It's like a real competition with shin pads, headgear, sparring gloves. …

Q: But it's not an official fight.
A: It's not official, but it's against another gym. They do the walk-in, and there's usually a small crowd. It simulates the atmosphere of a fight. A lot of guys find out whether they want to be out there. Even though it's three two-minute rounds, I guarantee you every guy who goes out there for the first time is going to be pretty damn tired.

Q: Does that help prepare him for five-minute rounds?
A: Yes, especially when you take a wrestler out of his element. Wrestlers are not very comfortable when they can't take a guy down. It forces them to strike. But it's no big deal because a loss doesn't count against their record.

Q: How would you improve his conditioning?
A: I'd do a lot of sport-specific stuff and circuit training, hit the weights and hit the bags with running in between. I'd do plyometrics—explosive training with a lot of jumping drills. I'd do sprints and interval work. I don't believe in long-distance running, what old boxers used to do. This isn't a marathon. I'm trying to get explosive power over a period of 15 to 25 minutes. I'm trying to develop his ability to have that explosive power for five minutes, [then] have it again after a one-minute break. I'm not trying to build a powerlifter, a guy who can push a bunch of weight one time. I want him to push a decent amount of weight over a long period. So I'd do a lot of explosive stuff with the legs, core-body exercises, jump squats, walking lunges and Pilates-type stuff.

Q: Do you have a way of rooting out bad habits in the people you train?
A: It's easier to start with a guy who's never struck before than it is with someone who's been fighting a lot. What happens is you get him all cleaned up in the gym, and as soon as the fight starts, it's back to what he knew because the adrenaline's going. A lot of that comes down to keeping an eye on him when he's training. You try to change things over time.

Q: Do you find that fighters learn from their mistakes better when they experience a loss?
A: That's the worst way, but they should learn from every fight they're in. The best ones are the close wins, where they know they didn't fight that well and they made a lot of mistakes, but they got out of it with a win. They do learn a lot from losses because that's when they have to look back and say, What did I do wrong? Usually, I wait a week or so after a fight to talk to my guys about it. I give them a little time—if they won to celebrate, and if they lost to get over it a little bit—before we watch the tape.

Q: What methods do you use to get a fighter to stay on track when he's facing an aggressive opponent?
A: We do a lot of situational stuff, but basically good sparring is where he'll get that. That's why I [mentioned] the smokers—getting a guy who is

a wrestler to learn how to strike. If he's doing just mixed-martial arts stuff, a lot of times as soon as [his opponent] comes in, he's going to take him down, and he'll never learn to strike like that.

Q: How do you prepare a striker to function on the ground?
A: Sometimes it's tougher to teach them the ground stuff, but a lot of guys from boxing have good athletic ability, and it doesn't take long to teach them counter-submissions. They have to be willing to put the time in. They're not going to like it at first because really good boxers are used to winning. They get to [an MMA] gym and there are guys they probably won't be able to beat for two or three months. It's frustrating, but they have to do it.

Q: How do you prepare wrestlers for getting hit?
A: That's one of the hardest things. A lot of wrestlers are gun-shy. Nobody likes getting hit, but it affects wrestlers in a negative way when they're not taking shots well. The only real solution for that is sparring—getting them in there enough so they feel comfortable moving around. There are other things we do: We have a glove on the end of a stick that we use to get them used to being hit and moving out of the way. Sometimes I hit them hard with that glove.

Q: In the education of a fighter, how important is the ability to live with pain?
A: Guys that make it to the top of the sport have gone through a lot of injuries and have been able to push themselves through being hurt in practice. This is one of the hardest sports in the world to train for and not get hurt. I don't think I've gone into a fight at 100 percent in a long, long time. I tell people there are no magic moves that will make them better at this sport. They need to be born with some athletic ability and be able to take a punch. It's hard work.

Q: What importance do you place on image as a factor in a fighter's success?
A: Image plays a bigger role than I would like it to,

but promoters want to sell tickets. People have to want to watch the fight. Whether they want to see you lose or win, as long as they want to see you, promoters don't care. It brings in more money.

Don't get me wrong: In this sport, if you're the best in the world, you can still make it as long as you're not losing. But you need to be exciting in the ring and somewhat exciting outside the ring.

Q: What general advice would you give an up-and-coming fighter?
A: Try to finish your fights. When it comes down to it, fans and promoters want guys who try to finish their fights. Even if you win every fight you ever have by decision, as long as you're trying to finish the fight, no one will have a problem with that.

Q: Does finishing a fight include fighting hard even though you're losing?
A: Right. Don't give up in any way and always be trying to win. In some fights, a guy gets a lead and just sits there and holds his opponent. Or in boxing, a guy gets a lead and just dances around for the last two rounds without trying to finish. People don't want to see that.

Q: What can you do to keep a fighter from freezing or losing focus when the lights are bright and the crowd is noisy?
A: The biggest thing is experience. What I try to do the first time they're in a bigger show is get someone they should be able to beat pretty easily. That way, if they do freeze up a little bit, it's not going to cost them the fight. Even guys who freeze up usually settle down after a round. If they lose one round, they have two more to win, so there's time. But if they go out there against an equal and freeze, most likely they're not going to make it out of that first round.

Q: In a fighter's training, how important is sleep?
A: When he's training hard, he needs his sleep because his body needs to recover. I don't worry about sleep when I'm not training, but when I have a fight coming up, I need my sleep.

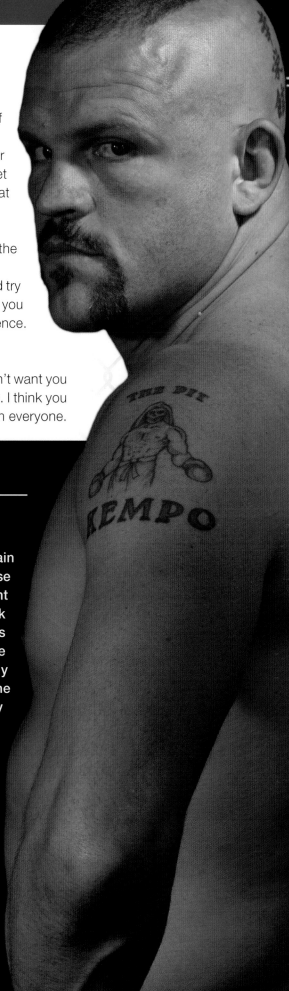

Q: How does a person's diet change when he's in and out of training?

A I eat. When I start training again, I start a diet with broader guidelines, but it's a lot cleaner than what I was eating. When I get down to the last eight to 10 weeks and I have to cut my weight, what I eat is very specific.

Q: It's tough enough to monitor yourself, but how do you control the diet of your fighters?

A: It's not easy to eat right. I try to tell them what they should do and try to get them to do it. A lot of them make a good effort, and that's all you need. A few slips here and there aren't going to make a big difference.

Q: Do you have any final advice for aspiring fighters?

A: Find a place that lets you train in everything. Some [coaches] don't want you training with other people and don't want you learning other things. I think you should get with somebody who's not afraid to have you learn from everyone.

THE RIGHT STUFF

by J. Michael Plott
Black Belt March 2005

The selection of Randy Couture and Chuck Liddell to captain separate teams for *The Ultimate Fighter* was perfect because of their skills and experience, said Dana White, the president of the Ultimate Fighting Championship. "Randy and Chuck will have complete control over every aspect of each fighter's training. We also have three assistant coaches who will be completely neutral in the competition and who will assist Randy and Chuck in any way they desire. One is a boxing expert, one a *muay Thai* expert and one a mixed-martial arts expert. They will take direction from each team captain and do just what they're instructed to do."

Couture and Liddell are at the top of their game right now and are arguably the best fighters in the world, White said, and that will benefit the TV series, as well. "They are also competitors for the same title and will likely face each other in a title fight in the near future, so the competition between them, though very honorable, will be particularly fierce. It should be interesting to see how much of their fighting styles and philosophies are reflected in their teams' fights. It's sort of an extension of old-school martial arts when a famous master would challenge another master to a test of skill, not only between themselves but also between their students."

JEAN JACQUES MACHADO

Worst-Case Jiu-Jitsu

Six secret ways to turn the tables on an opponent who's about to submit you!

by Robert W. Young, photos by Rick Hustead
Black Belt November 2008

Ever since the mixed-martial arts revolution began in the mid-1990s, more and more martial artists have seen the light and started learning the most common finishing techniques of the standard-bearer of grappling, Brazilian *jiu-jitsu*. A plethora of qualified instructors are ready, willing

and able to teach them the best ways to choke, armbar and leg-lock their opponent until he taps like a baby.

And that's fine.

What isn't so good is that most of those instructors give their students only what they ask for—which is flashy finishing techniques. In reality, what students need just as badly is a crash course in escaping from those holds in a way that places them in position to immediately execute a finishing technique of their own.

For expert instruction in the fine art of escaping and reversing, we sought help from sixth-degree black-belt Jean Jacques Machado. A member of the legendary Machado clan—he's the brother of John, Rigan, Carlos and Roger—Jean Jacques won just about every major jiu-jitsu title while competing in Brazil from 1982 to 1992, plus a bunch in the United States after moving here in 1992. Among his most prestigious victories were his first-place finishes at the Abu Dhabi Submission Wrestling World Championships in 1999, 2000, 2001 and 2005.

When Machado visited the *Black Belt* photo studio, we tasked him with devising an easy-to-learn escape that will extract you from seven bad situations, then enable you to turn the tables and finish your foe. The article in this book teaches two of them.

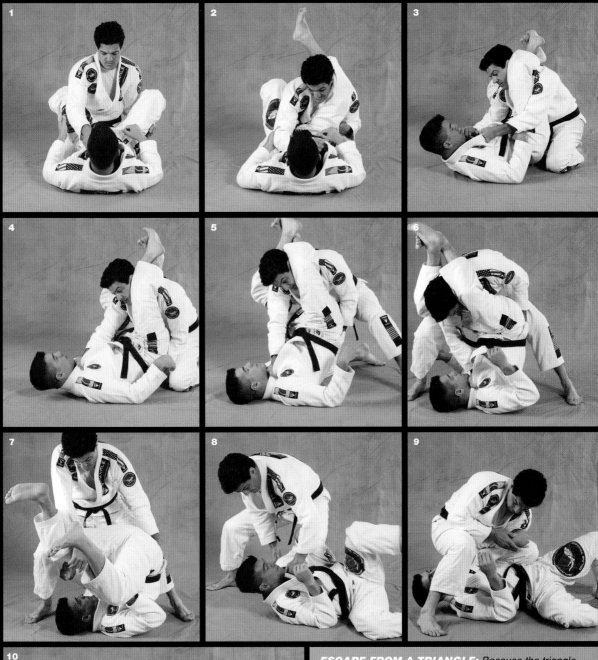

ESCAPE FROM A TRIANGLE: *Because the triangle gives the martial artist a chance to catch his opponent with a choke and an armbar at the same time, it's crucial to know how to nullify it. To prevent his adversary from using his whole body to execute the technique, Jean Jacques Machado keeps his head high (1-2) as he grabs both lapels with his right hand (3). He then uses his left hand to hold the back of the man's belt (4) and pushes forward to elevate his legs (5). Machado simultaneously steps toward his trapped arm—in this case, to the right (6). (Moving to the left would expose him to an armbar.) From there, he can use the collar to choke his foe, which causes him to release his legs (7-8). The opponent unknowingly leaves himself in position for an armbar (9-10) or a kimura.*

MACHADO IN ACTION

For full-motion instruction in the other techniques mentioned in this article—plus a bonus move—check out the Jean Jacques Machado video clips posted at blackbeltmag.com/machado-videos.

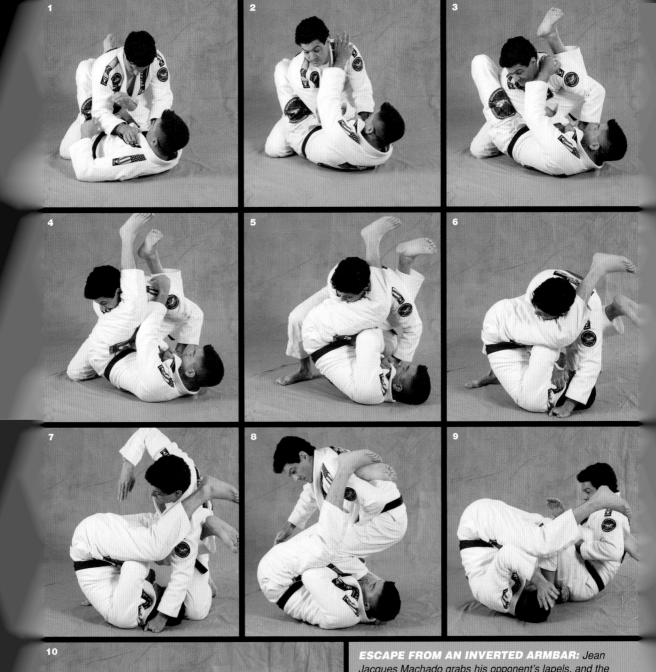

ESCAPE FROM AN INVERTED ARMBAR: *Jean Jacques Machado grabs his opponent's lapels, and the man immediately traps his arm (1). The opponent grabs his shoulder (2), shifts his hips and repositions his legs in preparation for an armbar (3-4). To neutralize the technique, Machado must vertically align the man's heels and knees (5), which stacks the two bodies so all the weight is resting on the opponent's neck and shoulders (6). Because there's nothing behind his right shoulder, Machado can yank out his trapped arm (7). He then grabs the man's right leg (8) and falls backward (9). With the ankle locked under his arm, Machado hyperextends the limb for a kneebar (10).*

JOHN MACHADO

3 Facets of Grappling

John Machado explains why you need to know them all.

by Robert W. Young, photos by Rick Hustead
Black Belt June 2007

As more and more martial artists recognize the value of augmenting their self-defense skills with grappling, we at *Black Belt* thought an overview of the various categories of techniques was in order. So with help from Brazilian *jiu-jitsu* master John Machado, one of the top grappling authorities in the United States, we offer the following examination of the big three: pain-compliance techniques, breaking techniques and choking techniques.

Man, That Hurts!

"Pain is one of the tools available to you in grappling, but it has limitations because a lot of people don't feel pain," Machado says. "Sometimes when you try a pain-compliance technique on someone's arm, leg or neck, he'll feel nothing. He doesn't have to be drunk or on drugs; he just doesn't feel it."

Fortunately, pain-compliance techniques work most of the time—approximately 70 percent, Machado estimates.

The majority of the moves function by crushing a muscle or extending a joint in an uncomfortable direction, Machado says. "The biceps lock works by 'cutting' the muscle. Another technique might work by extending the elbow, knee or neck to cause pain. The side neck crank is a good example. You don't want to break the neck; you want to cause pain by hurting the neck muscles."

In schools that teach leg locks, the calf crush is a popular pain-compliance technique. "You can do a foot lock on the ankle, or you can hold the calf and 'cut' it," Machado says. "A lot of people will tap right there. Just remember that for some, there's no effect."

He advises martial artists to avoid spending an undue amount of time trying to make a pain-compliance technique work. "When you apply a hold, watch your opponent's reaction," he says. "If you see him lifting his hand to tap, it's a sign the lock is working. Otherwise, quickly move to a different hold."

During that short period in which you're gauging the effectiveness of the move, limit the amount of effort you exert. "You shouldn't go 100 percent because you never know for sure that the lock is even going to work or whether he'll counter it," Machado says. "You should apply the technique and use enough pressure to make it work. You know from practicing it in the *dojo* how much force that requires—how much effort it takes in a perfect situation. If it doesn't have an effect, just move on."

Pain-compliance techniques will serve you well in training and self-defense, Machado says. Before you try them in a tournament, though, find out if they're permitted.

There Goes the Arm!

Breaking techniques target the body's joints, not the bones. Some of them are so cleverly designed that they attack more than one body part at the same time.

"When you do a triangle choke, for example, you're doing a neck crank, a choke and an armbar," Machado says. "You can finish your opponent with all of them together.

"The *kimura* usually targets the shoulder, but it can also attack the arm with an inverted armbar. It depends on the angle."

The most efficient breaking techniques use both of your arms against one of your opponent's limbs. The strength differential makes it relatively easy for you to hyperextend the joint, rupturing the ligaments and even breaking the bone. "The techniques are even more effective when you have your whole body working against one joint—whether it's a knee, wrist or elbow," Machado says.

In breaking, leverage is everything. "Without it, you can't do the moves because jiu-jitsu is based on leverage," Machado adds.

Many attempts at executing one of the most popular breaking techniques—the cross-body armbar—fail because the fulcrum, or the part of your body against which the opponent's arm is forced, isn't slightly above the elbow. "If you do it that way, you don't have the lock," Machado says.

"You're putting pressure on the bone. You need to switch to a different technique quickly because if you don't, he'll escape."

Breaking techniques are good for self-defense, but before attempting one, you must determine whether the situation will permit you to safely execute it. "You don't want to use an armbar in a fight in a nightclub with hundreds of people around," Machado says. "Every technique has its place, and that's not the right one for an armbar."

Likewise, if you're in law enforcement, you probably don't want to take a suspect down and break his arm because of the legal issues involved, Machado says. "You'd probably be better off using a short armbar to make him cooperate with the handcuffing procedure or subduing him with pain compliance."

In epic battles, just how debilitating is a broken limb? "In any form of combat, you have to deal with adrenaline and the fight-or-flight reaction," Machado says. "Sometimes a person doesn't realize that his arm is broken until the end of the match, so he keeps on fighting back. That's why, in some respects, chokes are superior."

Wake Me When It's Over!

The fighting arts teach two types of choking techniques: air and blood. "You can suffocate someone to death if you squeeze the throat, or you can subdue him the right way, which is by squeezing the arteries on the sides of his neck so blood stops flowing to his brain," Machado says.

It's obviously imperative to learn the difference. "You should never do a choke against the windpipe because you can kill your opponent," he says. The key to making your technique attack the arteries is to make a V-shape with your arm and position his windpipe in the crook of your elbow, he adds.

Once you begin applying pressure, it takes about three to five seconds for unconsciousness to follow.

Blood chokes can be effected with your arm or your opponent's uniform. "Both are very important in grappling and very effective," Machado says. "The arm choke is powerful. You can do it while wearing a *gi* or while not wearing one, so it works in a variety of situations. You can be on the beach in Rio and get into a fight and choke someone out using your arms. Or you can be in a cage tournament and use the same move."

But the key to success in self-defense, he says, is learning how to execute the choke with the collar. "It's more useful because everybody is wearing something—a shirt, a jacket, a uniform," he says. "Even a T-shirt can work. There's a chance it'll rip, but if you know how to grip it deep and pull, you'll have a better chance of making it work. The thing to remember is, if you can get your hand in deep enough to grab the T-shirt right, you can probably do an arm choke. It's all about being versatile."

When it comes to choking, builders of bulging biceps beware: Skinny arms are easier to insert into tight spaces such as the gap between a resisting opponent's head and shoulder or chin and chest, and bony limbs make the constriction more immediate. "And if your biceps are too big, it's hard to even get your arms in deep enough," he says.

Self-defense caveat: Depending on the state or country in which you live, you may want to forgo all-out choking as a self-defense strategy because juries often misinterpret it as an attempt to kill. "It's better to use a choke to restrain someone than it is to render him unconscious," Machado says. "A choke is like a gun: You cannot use it on everybody who assaults you."

Believe it or not, there are people who are immune to some choking techniques, Machado says. "It's very rare, but I've encountered martial artists who cannot be choked out," he says. "One was a friend of mine in Brazil: Renaldo, an old-time black belt under the Gracies. When we would see him, he would say, 'Come and test your choke.' He would give us his neck, and we couldn't choke him because of the way his body was built.

"At my school in Culver City, California, I have one student like that. If you try a collar choke or cross choke on him, your grip will get tired before you beat him. With a full back choke, though, he'll tap."

If you ever encounter an opponent who's resistant to chokes, Machado says, follow the same principle described above and move on to an armbar or some other grappling technique.

MACHADO JIU-JITSU COMES TO COMIC BOOKS

by Edward Pollard
Black Belt September 2008

Promotional Art photographed by Edward Pollard

Creative Impulse Publishing has begun working with Brazilian *jiu-jitsu* exponent John Machado on a project called *Faixa Preta.* The name, Portuguese for "Black Belt," has been attached to a comic book about a story that takes place on the streets of Novo Rio, Brazil, in the year 2020. In the following interview, Machado talks about his involvement.

Q: What was your inspiration for *Faixa Preta?*

A: Real facts are my inspiration—things that happened in my life with myself and my family. The situations that we witnessed in our surroundings—what happens in Brazil. My inspiration is the Brazilian scenario.

Q: Why did you choose to be involved in a comic-book treatment of those facts?

A: I grew up reading comic books in Brazil—from Marvel to DC Comics. But there weren't many Brazilian characters. For me, it was almost like a dream to be in a comic book. And nowadays, the comic book is also a very powerful medium. It's an art form that can reach millions of people, from kids to adults. Imaginations fly when you read them. It becomes like a movie in your head. So it's very influential. Just look how many movies are made from comic books these days.

Q: What do you want readers to take from the story?

A: No. 1 is that it's a positive story but one that makes sense in the real world. Through the main character, we ask the question, How do you use the martial arts in your life? We are going to have all different situations where our character has to use his fighting skills—but not to be violent. Actually, there are nonviolent ways to prevail. We live in times of war, where real people are being killed every single day on a large scale around the world. I want my comic book to be a good vehicle for people to give them some happiness, to calm them. Our readers will look at this story and see real conflict between rich and poor. We're going to show all that in the comic in a good way, a light way—what's really happening right now in our world but set in the near future.

LYOTO MACHIDA

Tradition Rules!

UFC star Lyoto Machida makes old-school karate work in MMA.

by Edward Pollard, photos by Rick Hustead
Black Belt February 2009

A traditional martial artist can rise to prominence in the mixed martial arts by imposing his will on opponents while strategically avoiding their attacks. It's a strange juxtaposition and a novel approach to a sport that owes much of its popularity to the stand-and-trade heroics of champions like Don Frye, Wanderlei Silva, Chuck Liddell, Forrest Griffin and Anderson Silva. Those who brave the oncoming fists and feet of their foes often do so to prove that they can dish it out *and* take it. On the other hand, it's also the only way many mixed martial artists know how to fight. Punishment is something you give and receive, says popular wisdom. It goes with the territory.

Lyoto Machida doesn't play that game. The 30-year-old martial artist enters the octagon with the demeanor of a samurai walking into battle—and he emerges victorious. With an MMA record of 13-0, he's become a cause celebrated among a larger demographic of fight fans. His technical dismantling of everyone he faces relies on none of the head games or public spectacles that mark the typical high-profile match. That's admirable if you're a martial artist, somewhat less so if you just want to see Rock 'Em Sock 'Em Robots go at it.

A Web of Battle

Before he ever set foot in a cage, Machida learned the way of *shotokan* from his father, a fourth-degree black belt at the time of the fighter's birth and a seventh degree today. The second of four sons, three of whom practice karate, Machida is intimately familiar with the techniques and philosophy of his family's art.

Of particular interest to many who've watched him fight is his tactic of not letting his opponent strike him. "The distance and timing come from my karate," Machida says. "He can't touch me at all because if he does, I'm dead. A long time ago in Japan, when someone fought, he used a *katana.* If you were touched by one, it meant you lost an arm or your life."

Once you grasp that concept, you can more readily understand Machida's combat style. "I have to escape all the time," he says. "I keep my distance. When I put him in my timing, he has to answer to my style. I don't answer to his style." Anyone who watched his recent bouts with Rameau Thierry Sokoudjou and Tito Ortiz, two larger and more muscular opponents, saw how he drew them into his web of movement. He wrapped them tighter and tighter into his strategy until they were caught in his line of fire.

Reactions to Machida's way of fighting are black and white on Internet forums. People either get it or think he doesn't want to mix it up—or, even worse, that he's afraid of contact. It's a new concept for most people.

"My style is very different, but in every one of my fights, I've faced tough guys like Sokoudjou and Sam Greco, who are big and strong," he says. "But I'm not afraid. I'll fight anybody. It doesn't matter if he's heavy or has power because I can nullify that. Tito said I was running, but I knocked him down and fought him a lot. What did he do to me?

"People don't understand that my style is a martial art, not a street-fight [style] like the majority of fighters—there's no technique. Compare a [*jiu-jitsu* expert] like Antonio Rodrigo 'Minotauro' Nogueira to a fighter like Bob Sapp. When you see Nogueira fight, you can see him use the *omo plata,* the triangle and sometimes escapes. Fighters like Sapp are strong, but they have no technique. The majority of them are just punching.

"I'm a martial artist first, and that's very important. I can double-kick, I can punch, I can do whatever I want. If I want to do a spinning kick, I do it. If I want to do a front kick or back kick, I do it. I use my head, my brains and my strategy. I have confidence in myself and my style."

Family First

Despite appearances, the half-Japanese, half-Brazilian phenom enjoys the thrill of competition. "I love fighting with almost no rules to prove who's the best, who's the strongest," he says. While Machida stands 6 feet 1 inch tall, weighs more than

200 pounds and keeps himself in good shape, he doesn't have the profile of a bodybuilder or a guy who relies on muscle power.

When Machida began competing in MMA five years ago, he stopped entering karate tournaments because he didn't have time for both. He didn't quit karate, though. "I still train with my dad and my family and my brothers," he says. "Twice a week, I put on my karate *gi* and train with everybody."

The Machida family workouts focus on their interpretation of shotokan, which they've modified somewhat for MMA. The result is called "Machida martial arts karate." In the northern Brazilian town of Belem, where his father's school is located, the Machida name is well-known. Although the MMA star no longer teaches there because of his demanding training schedule, he spends a lot of time mingling with its 300 students. It remains a nurturing haven where traditional discipline, respect and honor are promoted and unbeatable technique is taught. It's no surprise that his confidence level is so high.

Train for the Impossible

The five hallmarks of Machida's fighting method are distance, timing, kick-punch combinations, karate sweeps and ground submissions. To master them, he has to push past his limits, often to the point at which his defenses run the risk of failing. "I train a lot with boxers and *muay Thai* fighters," he says. "When I'm very tired, my coach will put a fresh, strong guy in to spar with me, and I have to block him. Sometimes he'll get me. Then I'll clinch and work him for the takedown. I train for this kind of situation."

One of Machida's favorite attacks begins with a front kick. He immediately follows up with a punch, using the resulting shock as an opening for a takedown. In another one, he feints a punch, then kicks and sweeps. "I like to use combinations to confuse my opponents," he says.

A third strategy begins with Machida blocking his opponent's front kick. He momentarily traps the leg, then hits him with a spinning elbow before taking him down and submitting him with an armbar. When he does it, it's fast enough to

deserve slow-motion video replay. Without giving away any secrets, he explains the best time for using the sequence.

"I normally use it in the second or third round when [my opponent is] more tired and his reaction time is slower," he says. "His concentration and focus will be lower. It's good to catch him when he's thinking or reacting to something else. Sometimes I catch his ankle and lock his leg when he kicks me. That's when I use the scissor takedown. The block is usually a surprise to him—nobody expects it. I finish with the traditional armbar."

Machida's patient drawing out of an opponent requires extraordinary cardio capacity, so he makes an effort to fill his days with exercise. "I wake up at 5 o'clock in the morning and train in karate with my family," he says. "At 10 o'clock, I train in jiu-jitsu in a gi. In the afternoon, I run and lift weights."

When he's preparing for a match, the routine changes. "I wake up later because sleep is very important for recovery," he says. "I train in techniques at the gym with my brother from 10 to noon—he teaches me strategy. I spar two or three times a week. Every afternoon, I train in techniques. [There's] no strength training but a bit of weightlifting and running. Of course, I do a lot of cross-training."

The deeper Machida gets into explaining his fight preparation, the more apparent it becomes that the whole is greater than the sum of the parts. What he does in training isn't too out of the ordinary; what enables him to win is the way he puts it all together in the octagon.

When asked if he's adding anything new to his routine or planning to change any of his traditional techniques, he smiles broadly and chuckles. "Not really, it's pretty much the same," he says. "I'm undefeated, so why change now?"

RENATO MAGNO

Profile: Renato Magno

by Jason William McNeil, photos by Rick Hustead
BOOK EXCLUSIVE

When imagining the front lines of the mixed-martial arts' two-fronted assault on the worlds of sport fighting and entertainment, one might be forgiven for not thinking immediately of Santa Monica, California.

Sunny, slow-moving and surf-adjacent, Santa Monica embodies the very essence of the laid-back California lifestyle with its latte bars and vegetarian restaurants, inclusive. In the middle of this warm and friendly mix, however, the current and future stars of the mixed martial arts gather together with Hollywood's elite, a fair number of up-and-comers and amateur enthusiasts to train at a small, blue-matted *dojo*, unobtrusively signed

"Street Sports Brazilian Jiu-Jitsu."

They come to train with Renato Magno, a man who has made it his mission to lead the art of Brazilian *jiu-jitsu* into the 21ˢᵗ century. Tough as nails but with a quick and caring smile, Magno enjoys a reputation as one of the finest fighters and trainers to emerge from his native Brazil, a country that sometimes seems thickly forested with jiu-jitsu and *vale tudo* superstars.

He also likes to choke people. A lot. Really—he's famous for it. He recommends it. Lots and lots of choking happens at Street Sports. His students are some of the best choke-out artists in the world, but more on that later.

Staking a Claim

While still a young lad of 13 growing up in São Paulo, Brazil, Magno first encountered jiu-jitsu when his father, Carlos Magno, began training with (who else?) the Gracie family. Shortly after being introduced to the art of Brazilian jiu-jitsu and adding it to his background in judo, Magno began tournament competition and won a gold medal his first time out.

According to Magno, his formal judo practice quickly fell by the wayside as Brazilian jiu-jitsu became the young man's all-consuming passion. Magno is quick to credit his development as an athlete and as a fighter to the influence and training of Gastão Gracie Jr., Carlos Gracie Jr. and the Machado brothers.

It was at the urging of the Machados that Magno immigrated to the United States in 1991, coming to work as an instructor at their Brazilian jiu-jitsu academies.

In 1998, Magno struck out on his own, opening Street Sports Brazilian Jiu-Jitsu in Santa Monica, where he maintains a stable of about 100 fighters and students.

In addition to running Street Sports with his wife, Sabrina, Magno also serves as a defensive-tactics consultant for the Los Angeles Police Department. To date, he has taught more than 8,000 of the city's finest and was awarded a special citation for his outstanding service to the LAPD.

In addition to instruction in the fighting arts, the couple have developed a popular sports-nutrition and supplement diet program that numerous students at Street Sports swear by.

For Magno, a fightsport veteran of no small standing himself with more than a decade of Pan-American Game victories and numerous judo and jiu-jitsu competitions under his black belt, it's only natural that today's MMA hopefuls seek out his training to add Brazilian jiu-jitsu to their fighting arsenal.

"If you look at the bare framework of mixed martial arts," Magno says, "there is Brazilian jiu-jitsu. Ever since the foundation of the Ultimate Fighting Championship, when Royce Gracie became the first UFC champion, what set the sport apart from other fighting styles were the Brazilian jiu-jitsu elements: the ground game and the stand-up game that leads to the ground game. Even though the style of MMA fighting has changed since the 1990s, the foundation of Brazilian jiu-jitsu is still there. It's still at the heart of the sport, and anyone who wants to be a successful mixed-martial arts fighter has got to have some skill at Brazilian jiu-jitsu to be able to survive and win.

"That's what Royce Gracie did when he first showed the world Brazilian jiu-jitsu at the UFC 1. That's why no one at first knew how to fight against BJJ, because of the kind of game plan that Brazilian jiu-jitsu brought to martial arts competition—the stand-up game and the ground game—and no one knew how to fight against it. Pretty soon, people watched and learned and got some experience with Brazilian jiu-jitsu and began to develop strategies for how to fight against that kind of game plan."

Magno maintains that is when merely pitting "style against style" inside the octagon progressed to experimentation and cross-training, the evolution toward true, modern mixed martial arts began.

Speaking of the Gracies ...

It's perhaps an unfortunate fact that, to most of the world, Brazilian jiu-jitsu equals Gracie jiu-jitsu.

For most Americans, Brazilian jiu-jitsu and the Gracie name are synonymous, due in equal parts to their genuinely Herculean efforts at developing Latin America's version of the samurai fighting art and their equal (if not greater) devotion to the art of self-promotion. Indeed, it has been argued that the first few UFC events, groundbreaking as they may have been, were essentially pay-per-view infomercials for the art and merchandising of Gracie jiu-jitsu.

While it's true that Brazilian jiu-jitsu may have begun with the Gracie family, it certainly doesn't end with them. A thriving culture of *gi*-jacketed grapplers has sprung up in their wake, evolving into a thriving competitive culture that reveres the Gracie name but is not bound to it or by it. Just in the relatively small area in and around Santa Monica, Magno (and his old friends and training partners Jean Jacques and Rigan Machado) proudly represents the full spectrum of the jiu-jitsu culture of modern Brazil—and, perhaps just as important, the current Brazilian jiu-jitsu culture of modern America.

Northern Evolution

"What's interesting," Magno says, "is the way that Brazilian jiu-jitsu has changed … you know, really evolved, since it came to America."

In the same way that the Japanese *jujutsu* of the Esai Maeda, aka Count Koma (rooted firmly in early Kodokan judo and the traditional samurai unarmed fighting art of *tenshin shinyo jujutsu*) was unavoidably and irrevocably altered by its immersion in the grappling-friendly culture of Brazil, morphing within two generations into what is now recognized as Brazilian jiu-jitsu, a unique martial art unto itself, so, Magno maintains, has what might be termed "traditional Brazilian jiu-jitsu," as originally developed by the Gracie family, begun to further adapt and evolve as it is practiced in the United States by constantly training, experimenting and competing MMA combatants.

"Training in the United States and training for mixed-martial arts competitions," Magno says, "is actually making the Brazilian jiu-jitsu people better fighters."

A bold statement. When asked to elaborate, Magno again draws on the example of the early UFC events.

"In the first couple of UFC's when Royce Gracie was fighting and winning them, the rules were different than they are now, and they were wearing gi jackets," Magno says. "There were no time limits. They'd go on for 20 or 30 minutes with not as many rules, so Royce would lie on his back in the guard and just slowly work his game plan, wearing out his opponent and working the ground game until he got his opponent in the position he wanted him."

"Now the game is a different game. There are time limits, no one wears the jackets anymore, there's different techniques being used, and fighters have had some experience fighting against Brazilian jiu-jitsu. They know the ground game now, so the BJJ fighters can no longer fight like that. They had to move out of their comfort zone and learn to play a different kind of game."

Preaching and Practicing

Taking his own advice to heart, Magno doesn't just teach. Although there is certainly enough interest in Brazilian jiu-jitsu to keep a teacher busy just passing that art on to the public, he stridently maintains a rigorous training schedule of his own, keeping himself in fighting shape and taking advantage of the opportunities the United States offers to cross-train with great fighters of others styles, backgrounds and skill sets.

"Living in Southern California offers tremendous opportunities to work out with really great martial artists," Magno says. "The two main guys that I get together with and trade techniques and spar with are Dan Inosanto and Ray 'Boom Boom' Mancini."

Mancini, a former professional boxing champ, maintains an office near Magno's Street Sports dojo, so it was only natural that the two great pugilists would gravitate toward one another. So great is the men's mutual respect that Mancini has become a fixture at Street Sports, guest-instructing Magno's students in the "sweet

science" of fisticuffs, helping to add devastating punching skills to Magno's legendary toolbox of takedowns, ground skills, locks and chokes.

The Fine Art of Choking

No two ways about it, Magno likes to choke.

Wait, that's not right. Yes, Magno likes to choke—loves it, in fact—and can (and will) expound on the subject at great length, but there are certainly more than "two ways about it." Magno knows dozens of ways to choke out an opponent and can cite just as many reasons why he thinks it is often a good idea.

"There are a lot of reasons that I think choking is a great technique to perfect and use in competition and in self-defense," Magno enthusiastically explains. "That's why I emphasize it to my students and make sure they spend time perfecting all their choking skills.

"For example, when you're sparring or fighting in a mixed-martial arts setting. Maybe the other guy has very good striking skills. Maybe he's a better puncher than you or maybe you've never seen him fight and you don't know what kind of punches he has, but you don't want to get beat up a lot to find out. Well, the great thing about choking is that it's up close, and if a guy's going to punch you, he has to come in close. If you're a good choker, good at closing that distance and pulling the opponent into your choke, then he can't punch you and you can put him out very quickly."

Magno illustrates with a story: "When I spar with Ray 'Boom Boom' Mancini, there's no way I'm going to stand there and trade punches with him. He's the boxing champion for a

reason, and I know he's going to kill me if I try to trade punches with him, so my game plan is to never play the game he wants to play if I can help it: to neutralize his punching power by either staying out of range (but I can't beat him by just staying away from him) or, more effectively, by trying to pull him into a lock or choke. Even if we go to the ground game, Ray can still punch me pretty bad on the ground, so I prefer to get behind him and choke him out because I know that'll end the match and make him play my game instead of his. That's the way I can beat him, by choking him out."

Outside the relatively friendly confines of the sparring circle, Magno is a strong advocate of choking skills as a highly effective means of self-defense, as well. "I like choking for self-defense for a number of reasons," the master says. "For one thing, most people—unless they've had some wrestling or Brazilian jiu-jitsu training—are not used to being choked and will pretty much give up as soon as you put your hand on their neck. Most people just panic when they start feeling choked. They don't know what to do and get very scared, so they just give up.

"Second, it's a great fight finisher. When you know what you're doing, if you can get a choke on someone, you can make them unconscious very quickly. It completely neutralizes the attack. That leaves you free to get away or call the police or whatever."

Speaking of the police, that brings Magno to the next of the many reasons he likes choking: the American knack for litigiousness. "If there's a fight and the police come," he says, "if you've been standing there trading punches with a guy, it's going to look very bad. Everyone will be beaten up and bloody, and you'll both probably get arrested. Also, you might seriously hurt somebody by hitting him with punches and kicks and end up getting sued because of it later, even if the other guy started the fight. If you choke him out, though, the fight is over quickly, it's very clean and no one really gets hurt. You come off looking much better, and you have better control of the situation. It's harder to say you were trying to excessively hurt

the other guy, you just wanted to end the attack."

"That's why I have my students practice choking both for competition and self-defense," he confirms. "We train in the jiu-jitsu jacket chokes—the ones using the collar of the gi or another piece of clothing, where you get a really good deep grip and use that to apply the choke. We also train the chokes that are good for mixed-martial arts competition—the ones you see in the octagon—as well as the chokes that are good for self-defense on the street. If the other man isn't wearing a jacket, then you've got to go to something like a guillotine choke or a rear-naked choke. There's all kinds of ways to choke out an opponent. You just have to know what you're doing, practice all the different chokes and know how to work them into your game plan. Then you'll have a really powerful weapon to use whenever you need to."

REDBELT: BIG-SCREEN BJJ

I n 2008, the movie *Redbelt* opened in movie theaters nationwide. Telling the not-unheard-of story of a martial arts instructor (in this case, he teaches Brazilian *jiu-jitsu*) who only wants to be left alone to teach his art but is forced into a seedy world of brutal fightsport, the film had its origins in Renato Magno's training hall.

"There were two reasons the *Redbelt* movie was so successful," says Magno, in the wake of the film's DVD release. "First was, of course, the great screenwriter, David Mamet."

One could certainly do worse than having the award-winning screenwriter and playwright of *Glengarry Glen Ross* fame to scribe one's film. It didn't hurt that the famously "alpha male" Mamet is one of Magno's longtime students at Street Sports Brazilian Jiu-Jitsu.

So what does Magno believe to be the other reason for *Redbelt's* success?

"The reason we got the opportunity to show authentic Brazilian jiu-jitsu to movie fans is because the story dignified both the sport and the role of the instructor as he struggles to make a positive impact on the lives of his students," Magno explains. "Instead of having a lot of fighting, there was a real message there and a portrayal of what the art of Brazilian jiu-jitsu is and what the teacher-student relationship is all about."

Of course, one can't have a martial arts movie without some good, old-fashion throwdowns— and Magno reveled in the opportunity *Redbelt* offered to show Brazilian jiu-jitsu in all its glory

"Most of the time in movie fighting, they always want to show the very flashy thing, the very fancy thing that looks exciting but isn't real at all," he says. "In *Redbelt*, I had the opportunity to help pick the fighters they used in the film and got input on what the fights would look like so that they would represent Brazilian jiu-jitsu accurately to the world."

Just as he's always experimenting, evolving and expanding on his martial arts journey, Magno is looking to the future when it comes to Brazilian jiu-jitsu on the big screen.

"Now that *Redbelt* has been successful, we're thinking that for the next movie," he excitedly explains, "maybe if we can get some bigger stars attached, we can really have a chance to show something incredible to the movie fans."

Stay tuned!

—JWM

FRANK MIR

Head Games

Young UFC heavyweight Frank Mir uses muscle and mind-set to destroy his unfortunate opponents.

by Josh Gross,
photos by Sara Fogan
FightSport Fall 2002

QUICK FACTS

Name: **Frank Mir**
Hometown: **Las Vegas**
DOB: **May 24, 1979**
Height: **6'1"**
Weight: **240 pounds**
Record: **4-0**

Snapping arms and taking names, Frank Mir is as brash and exciting a fighter as the Ultimate Fighting Championship has seen in some time. However, get him away from the octagon and you'd have a hard time convincing the mama's boy to cruise his native Las Vegas strip—he'd rather talk Sun Tzu.

By the sixth grade, Mir was a 6-foot, 200-pound man-child blooming under the neon backdrop of Las Vegas. Odds were he'd be spending cash on sleazy strippers, cheap booze and two-dollar parlays inside some seedy sports bar far from the glittering lights of Sin City's tourist attractions. However, Mir's not as over-the-top as some would expect.

In reality, he is a well-adjusted, articulate guy with a penchant for slapping lightning-fast arm locks on helpless opponents and reading classic novels that discuss war strategy. Mir credits his maturity to his *kempo*-loving parents' anti-Ozzy Osbourne upbringing and the support of his tightknit group of friends. "A lot of people look at their goals, fears and mental strategies in life and you can trace it back to their childhood," Mir says. "My parents almost treated me like an adult when I was a baby. I mean, I got punished like everybody else, but when I did something wrong, it wasn't the fact that I did it wrong. It was the fact that my mind allowed me to go there. So [their idea was], 'Let's fix why you thought that was OK.'"

Crossroads

While he was lucky to have a positive support system in place, Mir admits that his surroundings could have influenced a much different outcome. "In Vegas," he explains, "if you're not into something, you don't have something you're passionate about, or you float around from party to party—get into drinking, gambling or whatever it is—you could get into trouble. It's a hard city to be in. People are [sometimes at] one extreme or the other."

When others floundered, Mir turned a passion for martial arts into his livelihood. The result has been nothing less than spectacular showings in the octagon. Bursting onto the scene at the UFC 34 on November 2, 2001, he injured Roberto Traven's left arm one minute five seconds into the fight when the Brazilian was too slow to react to an armbar.

Mir's UFC debut was only the third bout of his career, yet many pundits felt compelled to dub him a fighter with enough potential to give the best heavyweights in the world all they could handle. Five months later, at the UFC 36, those beliefs were upheld when Mir slapped an unorthodox shoulder crank on veteran Pete Williams only 46 seconds after the opening bell.

There's no denying his ferocity in the ring. Likewise, it's clear that Mir is Dr. Jekyll when he's not fighting and Mr. Hyde when the cage door is locked behind him. The bridge that keeps both halves from falling prey to the pitfalls of Vegas life and the temptations that entice many fighters is, undoubtedly, his commitment to martial arts.

"I hardly ever go out to clubs," Mir says, which is surprising considering the night life Vegas can deliver. "I'm almost to the point where I can't remember the last time I went to a club. I'm just a simple guy. I think martial arts is life. That's why I put so much into it. I'm always thinking about it, always reading about it, always wanting to hear what other people have to say about it."

The Journey

Mir's discipline and philosophy are products of living in a household where both parents taught martial arts. Respect was a big part of that background. Growing up under the principles of kempo, he later incorporated boxing, wrestling and Brazilian *jiu-jitsu* into his repertoire as he strived to expand his knowledge. The clash between traditional martial artists and those competing in mixed martial arts is well-documented; however, it was Mir's parents who guided him down the path he's currently navigating.

"To be honest with you," Mir says, "I didn't want to [start MMA]. I thought I'd learn more boxing

and my dad told me to learn jiu-jitsu. The whole philosophy with kempo is: 'It's not the water in the vessel, but the vessel upon the water.' Everything is about adapting, growing and not closing your mind off to any route just because you have preconceived notions of what it should be."

Roughly two years ago, Mir met Ricardo Pires and listened as the Brazilian jiu-jitsu black belt conveyed his beliefs on fighting. For Mir, it was very reminiscent of his father's philosophies.

"My father says that martial arts is a full circle," Mir explains. "There is no destination. The farther I keep moving around, the more I realize it's not physical. You have to have the body to maneuver, but the mind is where it's at. When Ricardo started speaking, the strategy wasn't like 'sweep here, mount here.' It was 'OK, if you mess with a guy here, he'll lose concentration [because] you're holding here and this should be open. If it's not, this is open.' Everything was mental strategy on how to defeat an opponent. That's how I wanted to incorporate my jiu-jitsu. I didn't want to beat you physically; I wanted to beat you mentally."

Mind Over Matter

When it comes to what makes for a successful fighter, Mir's concept is quite clear. "Everybody knows techniques," he says. "The difference between a champion, a good guy and a scrub is not the armbar [or] the choke. It's not a sweep the other guy doesn't know. It's the mind-set, and that's one thing Ricardo totally understood."

Mir's commitment to the psychological aspect of fighting seems to have paid great dividends. In his third professional bout, Mir fought and won in the UFC before his hometown fans. For him, preparation starts and stops with Pires and the Las Vegas Combat Club. Mir explains that he places himself in a mind-set that renders the training under Pires an exercise in reality.

"I start thinking of images that make me nervous," he says. "This or that makes me scared, and I get that feeling that most people have when they have to fight or are in a confrontation. I'm nervous and dealing with the adrenaline. So

that way, when I do fight in the cage, I'm comfortable. I've done it 100,000 times. I've visualized it; I've been there. Every day I train, it's the same sensation. Too many people are comfortable when they train, and all of a sudden someone says 'fight' or 'competition' and their stomach turns upside down. Well, it's like what have you been doing training? It's no different. An arm lock on the mat is the same as an arm lock when 10,000 people are watching—there's no difference."

Anyone who's seen Mir fight can attest to the level of emotional investment he delivers, as well as how much he expects from the man standing across from him. Mir says the almost-primal howl he delivered following his last two fights was just the release of pent-up energy held in reserve.

Perspective

In the sometimes-sparse UFC heavyweight landscape, Mir looks like the type of fighter and person who can add some stability. He entered the UFC hoping to "enlighten people about what martial arts were really about." In two attempts, the message seems to be reaching fans—and fellow fighters.

"There are just too many things that you have to sacrifice to be a martial artist," Mir says, "so that was pretty much the deciding factor for me jumping into the UFC—win, lose or draw. I have to do something that's a sacrifice. I'll put my own ego [and respect] on the line and see what I'm about."

Despite having avoided many of the pitfalls and vices many young men encounter growing up in Las Vegas, Mir admits to checking his ego at the door to maintain perspective. "The first time you start thinking you're at the top of the hill or start thinking that you can't be stopped, then you stop thinking about it," he theorizes. "Once you stop thinking about it, someone will come along and take you. Even when you're the champ, you have to think of where you're weak. When you think you're invincible, you get lazy."

KARO PARISYAN

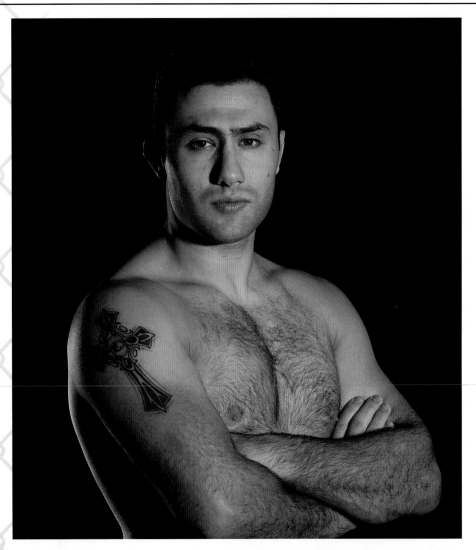

On Winning: The Youthful Wisdom of Mixed-Martial Arts Champ Karo Parisyan

by S.D. Seong, photos by Rick Hustead
Black Belt March 2008

Love him or hate him, Karo Parisyan is a force to be reckoned with in the mixed martial arts. A veteran of the Ultimate Fighting Championship, King of the Cage, World Extreme Cagefighting and several other promotions, he counts Matt Serra, Nick Diaz, Chris Lytle and Shonie Carter among his vanquished foes. He also was deemed worthy of facing Georges St.

Pierre and Diego Sanchez, and although he lost both bouts on the scorecards, merely being granted a shot at either one would be a huge accomplishment for any fighter. What makes the Parisyan story even more impressive is his age: He's only 25. In this article, the fighting phenom, who boasts a record of 25-4, shares some of his secrets.

On Preparation

Grappling is always there, so you have to make sure you have a solid base in it. I've been successful because I have my judo down, but I still polish it every now and then. You also have to be ready for ground and pound. Another part of the mixed martial arts you need to focus on is hands, both for boxing and for stand-up fighting.

On Hand Skills

I train in *muay Thai* and boxing. They're [used in combinations that flow from] kicks into punches. You don't have to train specifically to go out there and do a boxing match, but you should be able to make your opponent respect your stand-up, your power and your skills. If you can't initiate a takedown, you have to at least be comfortable when you're standing up until you can get into the clinch.

On Chokes and Locks

Chokes are good in MMA, but if you're into throwing like I am, locks are great because you'll have a "handle" on your opponent after he hits the ground. That makes it easy to maneuver his arm into an armbar or a *kimura*—or downward arm crank, as Gene LeBell says.

On Leg Locks

The legs are big targets, but a lot of times in MMA, leg locks don't work. In fact, they can be dangerous. If the guy escapes and stands, he can punch you while you're down. But it is what it is. Whenever I feel I can finish someone with a leg lock, I go for it.

On Finishing

It's fine to really push for a submission, but you have to realize that it's easier to lose when you do. Sometimes you put so much into a technique or you hold your breath while going for the submission that you get tired. That leaves you open. Then your opponent might escape and get positioning on you.

I've been fighting very safe because I really want the win. I didn't want to give my opponents an opportunity to get me in a submission or get positioning on me. In the past, that never really mattered to me, but now I'm fighting really tough guys. So I'm concentrating more on finishes that don't expose anything.

On the Hayastan Academy

When I left Hayastan, it had its pros and cons. I had more to gain [by leaving]. I gained because I got to train with better partners. I'm in a better mental state, and I have people wanting me to win, not people who think of me in a jealous way. My game has improved so much. I still have people around from Hayastan that want the best for me—they're my buddies—but I had problems with my coach, and that's the reason I left.

On Training Partners

For my last two fights, I trained at Xtreme Couture, Randy Couture's camp in Las Vegas. They're the best guys I've ever trained with. I also work with one of my students who became my training partner: Neil Melanson. He's a big guy, 230 pounds, all muscle—you need to work with someone like that for strength and conditioning.

If you're in MMA, you have to train with partners who are also MMA fighters. However, you should pay attention to what athletes in other sports do to improve their conditioning. The more you know, the better.

On Being in Top Shape

When you're in shape physically and can fight for five full rounds, you don't really have to care how in shape your opponent is. Mentally, you have to put yourself in the indestructible zone. I tell myself: "I'm going to do stuff to my opponent that he never even thought I would."

On Strategy

Have a strategy. For me it's simple: One way or the other, I will get my opponent into a clinch and throw him.

On the Unexpected

I like to come in from different angles. Passing

the guard, I'll punch my opponent and elbow him from spots where he won't see it coming. I'll go for a submission halfway, then stop and throw a hard elbow to give him a cut. Or I might ground-and-pound him into a submission—by hitting him hard and inflicting some pain on his body or face, then taking advantage of an opening and going for the finish.

On the Mental Game

The toughest part of fighting is the mental aspect. The brain is the strongest muscle. Your brain controls your entire body. If you're mentally broken or you're mentally not there, you can't perform to the best of your ability.

Preparing yourself mentally doesn't have to be overly dramatic. Before a match, I just train and pray that the outcome is good. I'm not a guy who throws up, turns blue and starts crying in the dressing room, saying I don't want to get out there and get my butt kicked.

On Octagon Experiences

When I fight, I don't really think that much. I like to break my opponent mentally. I like to stand in front of his face. Confidence and guts are the most important things. Don't back down. If you take a hard shot and then smile to show your opponent that you're not down, he'll think, What am I going to do with this guy?

I've given my opponents really hard shots, I've thrown guys and hit them hard, and sometimes it didn't affect them. That's where the confidence and guts come in. You still have to go after them. Think to yourself: I'll keep doing this until I win a decision. I'm not going to back down just because I think you can take my shots or my punches or my submissions.

On Staying Motivated

To be the best, you have to be smart and know the game. If you win and relax a lot, you're going to get bombed in your next fight. Even though each fight might not be harder than the last, you have to tell yourself that the more you win, the harder the fights are going to be. That way, you play it safe and always train your butt off.

On Losing

When you taste a loss, look at yourself in the mirror and see your cuts. Think about the depression you're feeling, how bitter and nasty it is. Then think about how you never want to feel that way again—all that emotional pain, that self-criticism.

Then, if you have to, go back to the drawing board. Get back on the horse and start riding again. The difference between a man and boy is that men don't give up at certain times and boys do.

My advice for the people around a fighter who just lost is this: We don't like to be pitied. We hate it when somebody says, "I told you that you should have done this." Don't say anything. Let us recover, then tell us whatever you want when we're in a calmer state of mind.

On His Big Losses

After the Georges St. Pierre fight, I was depressed. For two weeks, I didn't even leave my room. I take losses very hard because I have a lot of pride and a big ego. The Diego Sanchez loss wasn't really a loss in my opinion. I thought I won the fight, but still on the record it's a loss, and that stabbed me deep, too.

On Moving On

The best way to get over a loss is to go out with people who want the best for you and relax. Of course you'll be thinking, I don't want to be in that situation ever again. That's OK because it will motivate you to do whatever you have to do to win your next fight.

On Future Fights

At this point, I'm waiting to see who my next opponent will be so I can start training. If Marcus Davis wins his next fight, they might offer him. Or it could be Jon Fitch or Josh Koscheck. I would love to fight Matt Hughes because he's been the most dominating UFC fighter in history and because he's been the most dominating welterweight for

a while. I also want to fight Georges St. Pierre again. I have no animosity toward any of them, though.

On The Ultimate Fighter

I went to *The Ultimate Fighter* set to help my cousin, Manny Gamburyan, and his team. It was very good of the UFC and Spike TV to bring me on the show, to put my face and my name out there more. Any publicity is good publicity.

Unfortunately, I couldn't help Manny that much. I just grappled with him a little bit. I couldn't corner him. I thought Manny did great, though. I knew he would go to the finals. He's as tough as any of the guys on the show. Dana White didn't think that at the beginning, but he changed his mind after he saw Manny beating everybody's butt—no disrespect to Dana.

The finale was very unfortunate. Manny came out really bad with a rotator-cuff injury. He never wanted to take care of it—he was supposed to get surgery but never did. I couldn't believe it when I saw him tapping out. The guy's swimming in the whole ocean, and he drowned in a cup of water.

On TUF Athletes

I knew some of the guys that were on the show because they've been around for a while in the fight game. I had a little problem with one of the fighters, Nate Diaz. He showed me some disrespect when the cameras were on. I tried to joke with him and make him understand that you don't say that stuff when the camera's on. He walked away from me and tried to act tough. I said, "You idiot. If you want to act tough, stand in front of me and act tough." It was unfortunate and shouldn't have happened, but it happened and I'm just looking past it. I got my point across: Do not step on my foot because I will step on your head.

I don't get Nate and his brother, Nick, who I beat in the UFC 49. If you get your butt kicked, you get your butt kicked. What's your animosity? It's just a sport.

B.J. PENN

The Ultimate Fighter's Newest Coach Reveals His Training and Fighting Secrets!

by Edward Pollard, photos by Rick Hustead
Black Belt June 2007

In the world of mixed martial arts, it's not hard to spot a winner. He's usually holding a big, shiny belt and covered with sweat—and often the blood of his opponent. Some winners are different, and they find satisfaction in other ways. Take B.J. Penn, for instance. After making his mark in 2001 as a lightweight in the Ultimate Fighting Championship 31, he's fought in practically every weight class, including heavyweight, and has beaten tough opponents every step of the way. His biggest

recent win in the UFC came against Matt Hughes in 2004, who until then had ruled the welterweight division. Penn tested the waters of K-1 in Japan and Rumble on the Rock in his home state of Hawaii before returning to the UFC. In 2006 he fought a rematch with Hughes at the UFC 63. Penn dominated the first two rounds, then lost his momentum and the fight after an awkward injury. It was that loss, however, that cleared his schedule and allowed him to coach opposite his old nemesis, Jens Pulver, in Season 5 of *The Ultimate Fighter*. *Black Belt* spoke to Penn at the UFC training center in Las Vegas only days before the shooting of the hit reality-TV series wrapped.

Q: You were introduced to *jiu-jitsu* by Tom Callos. Did you feel that it offered you secrets for gaining more control in a fight?

A: I never thought about it as secrets; I thought of it as knowledge. I needed to know as much as I could at all times, and I always try to learn. I consider myself the forever student. I believe I'm the best, but I can never stop learning. You have to go to all the good people out there and learn what they know, whether it's swapping techniques or just being a straight-up student. Once you forget that, you're done. All you can do is train every single day and hope you're current with

what's going on because things move so fast.

Q: It must be difficult to stay current once you've risen to the top of the mixed martial arts. What methods do you use?

A: I train in jiu-jitsu all the time. I do some weights and some cardiovascular, and I stretch a lot and do plyometrics. Nutrition is important; you've got to eat the right foods. You've got to have a nutritionist or a friend who knows nutrition because if you're just working out and not eating right, you're wasting your time. Once you stop watching your nutrition, it ruins everything. Your body starts breaking down immediately. You have to combine hard training with proper nutrition. You learn so much faster because your brain functions better when it has better food.

Q: What's your training regimen when you're preparing for a fight?

A: I've done it all. I've gone six hours a day with three two-hour sessions. I've tried one hour a day. For this next fight [with Jens Pulver], I'm probably going to go three hours in the morning and an hour and a half at night.

Q: Do you tailor your training to your opponent?

A: No, it's just my normal 100 percent raised to a higher level. My 100 used to be one hour a day every other day, but now my 100 is train in the morning, sleep all day and train at night. I really like that long break in the middle.

Q: How do you develop your endurance?

A: There are different ways—the most basic is keeping your heart rate at 70 percent to 75 percent for a certain amount of time using a heart-rate monitor. I run on a treadmill, bike uphill or do whatever gets my heart pumping. Sprints are important for engaging the anaerobic system. I run laps underwater and do 500-yard sprints. I hate sprints, but I know I have to do them.

You can also do circuit training: sprint 40 yards forward, 40 yards backward, jump 10

...ASTER PLAN

...ome mixed martial artists adopt a strategy that ...entails fending off every attack their opponent ...unches while waiting for him to make a mistake. ...ce he does, it's time to exploit the opening.

...That strategy is fine, B.J. Penn says, but what if ...e other guy doesn't make a mistake? "That's when ...u have to force it on him. When you get good, you ...on't have to wait for him to make a mistake. You ...st force your will on him because you know his ...ptions are limited."

—*E.P.*

times, walk [in a] wheelbarrow 10 yards forward and 10 yards backward, jump off your hands left and right, then do skipping back and forth. Try to build your aerobic base and start working the sprints in. It's better to just stay in shape all year round and always be your best. When you drop out of it and then try to get ready for a fight in two months, you have to start all over. If your opponent's near your skill level and he stayed in shape all the time, he'll have the advantage.

Q: You're known for your flexibility. What role does stretching play in your workouts?
A: Every day I stretch about half an hour before going to bed. I don't stretch before practice; I just warm up to get the blood going. If I'm not too exhausted, I stretch after training. But often I'll go home, eat, relax, take a shower and then stretch before going to sleep.

A good routine is to start from your head and go down to your feet, stretching everything you want to stretch. Flexibility is essential. That's why so many people have such a hard time taking me down, passing my guard and reversing me when I'm on top. It's important to have strength with your flexibility. At the gym, you often see strong, stiff guys and weak, flexible guys. To become a force in fighting, you need to combine those.

Q: What's an average day like for you when you're preparing for a fight?
A: I get to the gym by 6 a.m. and get out by 9 a.m. so I can rest all day, like eight hours straight. Every couple of hours, I eat organic, healthy food—nothing processed. I focus on good carbs, no bad fats, low sodium and two gallons of water a day.

Q: How do you schedule your training around eating that frequently?
A: I wake up, drink a shake, go train for two hours, eat an orange to get my insulin level back up, maybe do an hour

of cardio, eat again, then just try to stay home. I might wait another two hours until I eat again, or I might come home and eat a cup of brown rice, six egg whites, a chicken breast or something like that. It all depends on the stage of my diet. If I'm trying to drop body fat, it might be a chicken breast in the morning, then tuna and rice with two cups of organic vegetables in the afternoon.

Q: How do you cut weight?
A: I just cut down on my food and try to make whatever I eat as healthy as possible. After 6 p.m., I cut the carbs, and then as I start getting closer [to the fight], I eat lighter things like rice and chicken, then maybe just fish and greens at night. Everybody knows: Cut the carbs and cut the fat, and you'll be looking good in no time.

Q: What if you've only got 48 hours to lose several pounds?
A: I don't like to do that, but a lot of guys do it. The No. 1 thing: Don't eat anything salty because sodium attracts water weight. Don't use sports

THE ULTIMATE FIGHTER SEASON 5

With the fifth season of Spike TV's *The Ultimate Fighter* under his belt, B.J. Penn is relieved to be able to return to Hilo, Hawaii, for some downtime before he begins training for his rematch against the show's other coach, Jens Pulver. In January 2002, Penn lost a majority decision to Pulver at the UFC 35 and let the championship belt slip through his fingers. The loss served as a catalyst for greater deeds, as Penn went on a six-win tear that saw Paul Creighton, Matt Serra, Takanori Gomi, Matt Hughes, Duane Ludwig and Rodrigo Gracie chalk up losses.

Penn claims the experience of coaching a team of fighters was like parenting. "Being on a show where so many people are competing in so many fights every day, I had to separate myself emotionally from it because it's an effort," he says. "During the first couple of fights, I was in an emotional knot. After a while, I accepted that this was going to continue for weeks and I couldn't put myself through that every day. It was one of the hardest things I've ever had to do."

—E.P.

drinks for the same reason. The week of the weigh-ins, flush your system by drinking two or three gallons of fresh water every day. You can lose more weight by sitting in the sauna and letting the sweat get all that salt out.

Q: Not many athletes are able to move up and down between weight classes. Why do you do it?

A: To me, that's part of what MMA is about. That's especially what jiu-jitsu is about—the little man being able to fight the bigger man.

Q: Do you have any favorite techniques that help you fight bigger men?

A: My game has hundreds of moves, and I do all kinds of advanced stuff, but I call what I do "advanced basic." I take the most basic moves and make them as advanced and as strong as possible. For example, if I'm grappling and I'm on bottom, I'm either going to sweep or submit you or stand up. If I'm on my back, I'll try a submission. If that doesn't work, I'll move on to sweep, pass your guard, mount, choke or armbar you. Anything that happens in between those moves, I'll take, but this is the way I try to go every time. When I'm fighting, I come in, punch you, grab you, put you down, pass, mount, choke, armbar. That's the game plan.

If I'm on my back defending from the guard and you're on top trying to pass or punch me, I'll look for a submission. It could be a triangle or arm lock from my guard, and if I can't get that, I'll look for a sweep to put you on your back. The guy on top controls everything. He controls the weight he's putting on you, and you're constantly pushing him away. Of course, I always want to be on top, but when I'm on bottom, I might try to go for one of the five sweeps I really know. The same thing applies to reversals.

Q: When you're on the ground, do you feel

any sense of urgency to win, or do you not worry because you have a great ground game?

A: When I'm on my back, I'll go for a couple of moves as quickly as I can. It's not like self-defense, where I can take my time. It's a sad fact of the sport that you're fighting the clock as well as your opponent. It takes away some of the purity of the sport and the martial arts, but that's today's world. You have to be in great shape to push and win.

Q: Which techniques do you think are most effective for MMA?
A: You have to learn all the different martial arts if you want to succeed in this sport. The three basic things to learn first are kickboxing, wrestling and jiu-jitsu. You have to build a base and a style so you have something to fall back on in case anything goes wrong in a fight. Your base is your instinct, and you build on it. Jiu-jitsu players add wrestling and kickboxing. If you're a kickboxer, add a good takedown defense and some jiu-jitsu so you don't get submitted easily if you do end up on the ground. Really, it's about making yourself well-rounded—in stand-up, in takedowns and on the ground.

Q: Your base is jiu-jitsu, isn't it?
A: I was introduced to it before wrestling. Jiu-jitsu is not the perfect martial art for beating today's high-level UFC athletes, but I still feel that it's one of the best self-defense arts. If you don't want to fight and some guy's trying to punch or kick you, you can still run away. If the guy chases you down and tackles you, you have ground-fighting skills. Jiu-jitsu's weakness is that a lot of players don't have good takedown defense, which is something you can learn from judo or wrestling.

Q: Which techniques do you find most effective?
A: I like to do chokes. Somebody who's caught in an armbar can let his arm break, but if you've got

TEACH AND TRAIN

No matter whom he's gearing up to fight, B.J. Penn manages to dedicate time to furthering his *jiu-jitsu*. "You don't know a move until you can teach it," he says. "I don't care how well you can do it; you don't really know it if you can't make someone else understand why it works."

Penn mentors students of all ages five days a week at his gym in Hilo, Hawaii. Does giving instruction help solidify the knowledge he already has? "It just gives me something to do in the daytime," he says with a laugh. "I never picture myself as a teacher. I'm just like another training partner there."

While he's traveling the world, he always makes an effort to train with the best jiu-jitsu, wrestling and kickboxing practitioners he can find. Most recently, he's taken pointers from Rigan Machado, Randy Couture and Matt Lindland. "If you stop learning because you think you know everything, you're making a big mistake," he says.

—E.P.

him in a choke, he's going to sleep. If I'm on top and punching you, I might go for an armbar, but most of the time I'm going for a choke.

From your back, you've got to be able to do armbars and triangles, too. With submission skills, you can extend your career. That's why it's important in MMA to save your body and protect your brain. You can win using armbars, locks, slams and takedowns. You don't need to punch each other in the face all day.

Q: Can you sum up your fighting strategy?
A: Go straight in and always give a higher output than the other guy. For anything in life, you should just do more than the other guy. No matter how much he does, you do more. Everybody can break, so try to break him mentally. If he throws five punches, you throw 20. If he throws 20, you throw 40. If he defends against 15 takedowns, you do 17. That's just what you have to do every single time you get in there. It's pretty tough to maintain that level, so you'd better be in shape.

BAS RUTTEN

Fighting Legend Bas Rutten Rates the Best and the Worst Moves in the Martial Arts!

Part One Through Part Three

by Lito Angeles, photos by Rick Hustead
Black Belt August 2007 through October 2007

It takes more than a few big wins to become a fighting legend. It takes a track record that spans years, if not decades. It takes experience in a variety of combat sports, including traditional martial arts, full contact and mixed martial arts. And it takes a skill base that covers all facets of fighting, from punching and kicking to clinching and grappling. Three-time King of Pancrase titleholder Bas Rutten is one of the few men who meet all those requirements. Once ranked No. 5 in the world in *muay Thai*, he owns a second-degree black belt in *kyokushin* karate and *taekwondo*, which means he's about as well-rounded as they come. In this exclusive interview, Rutten offers his perspective on the ring and street viability of the most common martial arts techniques.

Q: Let's start with the jab. How useful is it in mixed-martial arts competition?

A: It doesn't work because MMA has takedowns. Many people—including any good wrestler like Mark Coleman—will eat a jab to take you down because it has no power. The jab works nicely in boxing because there are no takedowns and it works as a setup in Thai boxing but not in MMA.

In the Bas Rutten system, I call my version of it the "left straight." My body stance is different—it's not on one line, which allows me to hit harder by turning my whole body. You'd better block the left straight because if you don't, you might get knocked out. You don't have to care too much about the conventional jab, though, because it's thrown from a boxing stance, which means it doesn't have much power. It's powered only by the puncher's arm.

Q: And the jab in self-defense?

A: Worthless for the same reason—unless your opponent is a striker. In a street fight, you don't know anything about him. He could be a boxer, wrestler or submission fighter. So don't take the risk.

Q: You said you teach people to use a square stance so they can put more power into their jab, or their left straight. Doesn't that leave them more vulnerable to a body shot?

A: I've been doing it that way for 20 years, and I've never been knocked out by a body shot. It's all in how you train. If you stand in one line, you have no power in your left hand, and there's no power in your left kick. If you stand square, you're a bigger target, but because you're aware of that, you're more defensive. And all your offensive and defensive techniques are stronger. I'd rather have all the benefits and put up with one negative. More and more boxers are using the square stance.

Q: Next is the right cross.

A: I call it the "right straight." It's great for MMA as long as you time it right. It's a hard punch, so your opponent needs to block it. Any technique that forces your opponent to block first is good because it slows down any takedown attempt

that might come afterward.

For self-defense, the right straight is very effective. In the fights I've been in, 90 percent of the time it's what I used to knock out my opponents. When I was a bouncer, my opponents would usually come in with a big right hand; I would just let them miss, then counter with a right straight. If I had to pick one technique for the street, this would be it.

Q: What's your opinion of the lead hook?

A: If you stand in a square stance, it can be very effective in MMA. If you stand in a line to make yourself more compact, you need to load up before you can do a left hook. Look at the match between Jens Pulver and Duane Ludwig. Ludwig was the first guy to knock out Pulver. Because Pulver stands in one line, we knew that he was going to load up his punch. I told Ludwig, "If he does that, hit him with a right straight." That was the first punch that sent Pulver down. Everybody who stands in one line and opens with a hook telegraphs.

Q: Do you advocate using the lead hook for self-defense?

A: Same thing. If you stand in a square stance, it's good. If you don't, I wouldn't do it.

Q: What about the rear hook? Some boxing commentators don't even acknowledge the technique. …

A: It's very underestimated. It's a good punch. A left straight–right hook to the head works so good.

There's something I need to add about hand strikes: In MMA, it's legal to hit with the open hand. So I like to hit with my palm—not my hand but the bony part near my wrist. If I'm fighting a tall opponent, using the inside of my palm gives me a longer reach without sacrificing effectiveness. If I hit him behind the ear with the bony part of my palm, he's going down. And hitting him in the head with my palm keeps me from breaking my hand.

Q: Don't you think it's hard for the average person

to decide whether he should use the palm or the fist while under pressure?

A: Yes, which is why many people choose to go with just the fist.

Q: What about using the rear hook for self-defense?

A: It's exactly the same thing.

Q: The overhand strike with the rear hand seems to be the "in" punch in MMA—Randy Couture used it to beat Tim Sylvia in the Ultimate Fighting Championship 68.

A: It works real well. It's more of a hook that comes down and hits with the two knuckles. Fedor Emelianenko uses it very effectively. I love it.

Q: Rich Franklin recently threw an overhand strike off the lead hand. What do you think of that?

A: A normal straight punch goes in between the opponent's defenses. An overhand goes to the side. It's almost the same as a hook, but it goes farther. There's a chance that you'll break your hand—I believe that Emelianenko broke his twice already because of the overhand right. The bones of the hand aren't lined up well in this punch. If you hit straight, it's OK to hit with the two knuckles but it's preferable to hit with the middle one. But with an overhand strike, you should use just your index-finger knuckle because it's aligned with your arm.

Q: Does the overhand strike work for self-defense?

A: It's very effective. In general, all punches that work in MMA also work in self-defense. With submissions, it's different.

Q: Next on the list are the lead uppercut and rear uppercut.

A: I love them because nobody uses them. I love the left uppercut–right straight and the left uppercut–right hook. Or the left uppercut with a right hook to the body.

Q: What about doing the uppercut with the rear hand?

A: It's more difficult to land, especially if you just throw it. Most of its usefulness is in the clinch or when you've set it up first, maybe with a left hook. It's dangerous to lead with the rear hand when using an uppercut.

Q: When using the uppercut for self-defense, is there an increased danger of breaking your hand?

A: Not if you do it the right way and hit the jaw. The way I do it, my opponent cannot escape. If he's in front of me and I throw a right uppercut, I hit the back of my hand against his chest and slide up and under his jaw. If you do a normal uppercut and go straight up, all he needs to do is move his head back a little to make you miss. The way I do it, he can pull his head back if he wants, but because my hand slides up his chest, it always connects.

Q: And for self-defense?

A: I would normally use a right uppercut after leading with a left hook.

Q: Are there any other hand strikes that you've found to be effective?

A: The left hook to the body. I've dropped a few guys in fights with that. I've knocked out hundreds of guys with it in training—usually in the form of a liver shot.

Q: Is the right hook to the body as potent?

A: It is, but it's easier for the opponent to detect. Still, a lot of people underestimate it and don't think about it. But I'd say the left hook to the liver is more effective. A good combination is a right uppercut and a left hook to the body. It looks like you're too close to do it, but you're not. The combination is great for self-defense, too.

Q: Some of the hand strikes we discussed are easy for the average person to do, but some are difficult. What would you advise novices to focus on?

A: Uppercuts they automatically know. A lot of people do the hook the wrong way, making it more of a combination of a straight punch and a

hook. The hook is effective only if it can bypass your opponent's defenses. So I would advise martial artists to concentrate on their straight punches and especially on the proper way to make a fist. Unlike what many books teach, you can't fight with your hands clenched all the time because you'll waste too much energy. You should squeeze them tight only at the end—to make your fists solid at the moment of impact. Otherwise, you'll break the bones in your hands.

Q: What are your views on the subject of palms versus fists? When you were in Pancrase, you were unbelievably effective with your palms. What is your preference now?

A: It depends on whether I'm on the street or in the ring. In MMA, I'll use my fists because they're very effective and they're protected by gloves. On the street, it's palms because I don't want to break my hands. I fought a lot as a bouncer, and I used a lot of palm strikes. So when I started using them in Pancrase, they said I was a natural. My first opponent was taller than me, and that was a perfect time for a palm to the jaw. It was my first knockout in MMA. To the body, however, it's always fists.

Q: Next is elbows. Personally, I think they're overrated in stand-up. Even in Thai boxing, you don't see many elbow strikes. In a clinch, it's once in a blue moon. When one hits, it doesn't do much—maybe open a cut. What's your opinion?
A: Everybody says they want to make MMA as close to a street fight as possible. That's why we don't have an eight count—if you're dizzy, you're going down. Well, then, they should take elbows out. On the street, if I get hit in the eye and get cut, I won't stop. It's not a knockout; it's just a cut. But in MMA, they stop the fight.

Elbows cut people. How many people get knocked out? Almost none. A lot of fighters will put their opponent against the fence and start rubbing their elbows in his face, and he gets cut. And they'll win because of that cut. I don't see that as a victory. That's why I'm happy that the International Fight League took elbows out.

Also, if you're working circles around your opponent for two and a half rounds and then get cut by his elbow, I don't think it's fair that the other guy wins.

Q: What about elbow strikes for self-defense?
A: It depends. A lot of people don't use them the right way. On the street, if people don't know much about the martial arts, it's easy to knock someone out. Standing, the chances are way less, but in a clinch, you can do a lot of damage with an elbow. A lot of people get intimidated when they see blood. On the other hand, some people get angry if they get cut, and that makes them fight harder.

Q: Regarding specific elbow techniques, what do you think of the downward diagonal elbow to the neck?

A: Do you know how difficult it is to hit someone in the neck when he's in a fighting stance? It's cool if you can hold one of his hands and go over the top with an elbow. But again, if you cannot create a lot of distance, it's not as powerful.

Q: What about the spinning elbow?
A: It's a waste of time. Turning your back to your opponent is dangerous. If you're fighting a Greco-Roman guy and try to do a spinning elbow but miss, you're flying. And then it's over.
On the street, a spinning elbow could be effective because you probably won't be fighting a professional. But generally, you don't want to turn your back on your opponent because of the risk. The same goes for the spinning back kick. Don't get me wrong: Some guys can do a spinning kick to the head and be so freaking fast—plus the leg is longer than the bent arm. But those people aren't the average Joe.

Q: Let's start with knee strikes—the upward shot to the head, the knee to the thigh and the diagonal knee to the body. Do you think knees should always be thrown off the rear leg?
A: Yes. If you do them with your lead leg, it's a waste of time because you can't create any distance, which you need to generate power. Without switching your hips first, you can't knock him out—unless you're lucky, and I'm not a gambler. Plus, because the strike isn't hard, your opponent can grab your leg.

In mixed martial arts, always aim your knees for the head. If you go for the body, your opponent will probably be able to absorb it once or twice, and one of those times, he can grab your leg and take you down. But with a knee to the face, he has to defend first before trying to grab it, and that gives you an extra beat to get out of there.

Q: Are there any other good targets for knee strikes?
A: Knees to the thighs are very underestimated. They're effective in MMA and self-defense. I had a 200-pound student who was preparing to

face a 400-pound guy in a cage fight. He asked me, "What am I going to do?" I said, "It's very simple. Close the distance, clinch, slide under his armpit to his back, wrap your arms around his body and start kneeing the back of his legs—his hamstrings."

My student gave him three or four knees to the hamstring, and the guy dropped. Then my student mounted him, and it was over.

The key is making good knee strikes, not the crappy ones many people do with their upper thighs. Use your kneecap, not your upper leg. Keep your hips back so you can create distance, and don't throw your hips and knee forward at the same time; many people do this, but it has no power. Move the knee first, and to add your weight to it, thrust your hip forward at the moment your knee hits him.

When you're on the ground, you can also throw knees to the legs. If your opponent is on his back and you're in side control, load up your knee—all the way back—and use your kneecap to hit his thigh. Two shots and it'll be over because when he's on his back, he can't flex his legs to absorb the power of the strikes.

BAS RUTTEN DOCUMENTARY

by Edward Pollard
Black Belt May 2008

Bas Rutten's new MMA documentary, *Potent*, sets out to answer the question, What makes a champion? Eschewing the trash talking and over-the-top hype of today's fight promotions, *Potent* emphasizes the "art" in the mixed martial arts by exploring the cerebral side of the sport with many of MMA's greatest innovators and pioneers, including Dan Henderson, Frank Shamrock, Mario Sperry, Vitor Belfort and Dean Lister. The film weaves together interviews and behind-the-scenes training footage that captures the mental toughness and creativity fighters need to succeed in the ever-evolving sport.

Q: The upward knee, diagonal knee, roundhouse knee—in your view, they're all useful?
A: If they go to the head or thighs, yes. The general rule is, if you're fighting a striker who's not going to go for a takedown, you can use knees to the body. If you're fighting a wrestler, don't throw a knee to the body because he'll take it, grab your leg and take you down.

Q: What about using knee strikes in combinations?
A: I like to mix it up. Some guys do left-right-left-right, but I prefer to do left-left-right-right or left-right-left-right-left-left-right. Or one knee to the front of the head and then the same knee to the side of the head. That can really throw your opponent off.

Q: You don't like alternating knees?
A: Look at boxing. A fighter will put someone in the corner and give him 25 punches—and 24 of them are defended because it's left-right-left-right-left-right, the same pattern. But if you go right-left-right and suddenly another right, you break the rhythm. It's the same in MMA.

Q: For self-defense, would you teach people to use a knee to the head?
A: Yes, if it's a dangerous situation, but normally to the body and legs. When I was a bouncer, that was my weapon of choice—along with low kicks and chokes. But if I was going against a real bad guy—someone who liked to hit women, for example—I'd knock him out. I tried to stay away from the face because when a person is drunk, it's not fair to do something that makes him wake up with teeth missing. He doesn't know what he's doing.

Kicking the legs is way more effective than trying to kick the head, and it's demoralizing for a person to lose after he's been kicked in the leg. He just falls to the ground and can't do anything. On the street, nobody understands the power of leg kicks—or how to flex or turn your leg to absorb that power. I don't recall ever having kicked more than once in a street fight when that kick connected.

Q: Specifically, what do you think of the side kick? You once said it's worthless in MMA.

A: For most people, it is. But there are a few people, like Don Wilson, who can pull it off—which he did in kickboxing. There might be only 10 guys on the planet who can do that, however.

If you want to use a side kick, go for the head. A kick that's thrown with power to the body is too easy to deflect and counter. Your opponent just steps a little bit out of reach and pushes your leg to the side, and you're left totally off-balance.

The only time I use the side kick in MMA is right after I throw a right or left low kick and miss—and because of the miss, I'm not squared up with my opponent anymore. Then I use it to keep him away. I never use it to go for a knockout. I've never seen a knockout with a side kick. I'm sure some people have done it, but not in the fights I've seen.

Q: How about the side kick for self-defense? Everyone learns the side kick to the knee.

A: I know it's in all the books, but again, I've never seen anybody kick someone in the knee in a street fight. That happens only in the movies. Maybe if your opponent on the street isn't ready and you kick him by surprise, or if you're facing the bar and one person comes at you from each side and they're also facing the bar. A side kick to one of the guys' knees might work because they're lined up for it, but you have to kick hard, and that means you really have to lift your leg up. He'll have to be really slow to not see that coming.

But if he stands in front of you in a fighting stance, I've never seen it work. It's the same as the myth of hitting an attacker's nose and shoving the bone into his brain.

Q: Next is the front kick.

A: It's very effective in MMA and street fighting because it keeps your opponent away from you. It's a great setup for something else. If somebody comes at you with an overhand right, put your foot up and execute a front kick—and he'll walk straight into it. Do this with your front leg but know

that you really need to train because the timing needs to be perfect. Your back leg is too slow for this, of course.

That kind of front kick was a good weapon for me when I was a Thai boxer. Everybody breathes in as he loads up for an attack. That's the moment he's most vulnerable in the abdominal region. You just thrust the ball of your foot into his solar plexus, and he's going down. He can do 3,000 sit-ups a day, and if you hit him with a front kick as he breathes in, he's going down. It takes a lot of training for the average person to have the necessary timing and accuracy, but practice makes perfect.

Q: What are your views on the rear-leg front kick versus the front-leg front kick for self-defense?

A: Both are good for setups. Of course, the rear leg is more intimidating because it's more powerful. To keep a person away on the street, kick him higher on the chest to make him fly backward. If you kick low and don't hit him in the solar plexus, his low center of gravity will absorb your power and he won't move. Also, people can absorb more of an impact when their lower abs are the target.

Remember that if you don't set up your kicks with punches, they can be dangerous to throw. Every kick can be countered because the legs are slower than the hands and because you're on one leg when you kick. You've got to be Mr. Perfect. If you're not, you give your opponent time to think a little bit, then act. I'd never use a kick on the street—except the front kick, which I'd use to keep an attacker away from me, and the low kick I just mentioned. Only two times did I use a head kick with success on the street.

Q: What are your thoughts on the roundhouse kick in MMA?

A: Again, if you set it up with a punch combination, perfect. Or if you're Mirko "Cro Cop" Filipovic, of course you can fire away.

When somebody is fresh, though, it's difficult to hit him with a roundhouse kick to the body

that has knockout potential. If he's tired, you may be able to pull it off because his reaction time is slower, but still try to set it up with punches. In MMA, when you fight a wrestler and go for a kick to the body, watch out! He'll take it and grab your leg. Look at what Kevin Randleman did to me in our Ultimate Fighting Championship fight: I kicked, and he used that to take me down.

Q: And the roundhouse for self-defense?
A: Chances are, on the street you're not fighting a professional fighter, so it might work. But I wouldn't do it because if you miss and are off-balance, he might run in and take you down. And what if that happens when you're fighting multiple opponents? It's better to use stuff that doesn't throw you off-balance so quickly.

Q: How about jumping and spinning kicks?
A: They're very difficult for the average person to pull off. Of course, if you're a champion taekwondo stylist who knows how to kick hard—not all of them do—and you're facing an opponent who doesn't know anything, you can probably succeed. In striking events, I saw many KOs with kicks like that, but in MMA against a wrestler? Maybe not. You can be fast, but if the wrestler shoots in, you'll be on your back. I always tell people to stay away from the tricky stuff unless their opponent is dazed from a head strike or is very tired.

Q: How do you approach kick defense on the street?
A: I like to let the person miss, or block his kick and counter right away. That attacks him mentally because if the kick is all he's got and you counter that right away, he knows he's done. Nobody kicks picture-perfect. When somebody kicks, there's pretty much always an opening, especially on the street. If he kicks, for instance, with a left roundhouse to the body, you can block and counter right away with a right straight. If you connect, he won't use that kick anymore.

Q:: Let's start with clinching and dirty boxing. These days in mixed-martial arts competition,

overhooks are used a lot more than underhooks because underhooks open you up to elbow strikes. What are your thoughts on that?
A: Using overhooks is good, but you've got to keep pulling him up or he'll shoot for your legs. If he's a wrestler, it's very hard to keep him away from your legs, especially when you try for an elbow strike.

For self-defense, though, you have to ask yourself, What kind of guy am I likely to encounter? If he adopts a Thai-boxing stance, I'll take the risk and use overhooks. But if he assumes a low wrestling stance, I'll probably use underhooks.

Dirty boxing is nice, but it's not that effective because it's very close-range. Have you ever seen anyone get knocked out using dirty boxing? It's good for setups but not for a knockout. It goes back to my rule: Once you close the distance, your punches don't have far to travel, and that means no power.

Q: Do you teach students of self-defense to either disengage from the clinch or take it to the ground—but to never just stay there?
A: Always. I teach people to get under the jaw, push him away, create distance and go for the straight punch. Of course, for guys like Dan Henderson, Matt Lindland and Randy Couture, who are good at Greco-Roman, fighting from the clinch works perfectly.

Q: In terms of fighting techniques for the clinch, what have you found to be effective?
A: Knees are best, but you first have to create distance with your hips. Never let your hips get close to his hips, or you won't be able to generate power. Hit with your kneecap and aim for the thighs. If you're skilled, you can do a straight knee to the head or a roundhouse knee to the head or body.

Q: If the average person winds up in a clinch in a self-defense situation, are knee strikes still the best bet?
A: They would work well. Or you could go for a

guillotine. The main thing is to create distance and get away. Without distance, you can't even strike.

Q: Speaking of the guillotine choke. ...
A: It's very good. I've used it to knock out guys while we were still standing. But I don't advise people to try the guillotine when they're facing multiple opponents. I used it once when I was taking on three guys, and I got kicked in the head. I still choked him out, but that kick could have been a stab with a knife. Remember that with any choke, you have no defense because you're using both arms. With multiple opponents, you have to complete the technique—if it's an armbar, for example, snap the arm—right away and get out.

Q: Shouldn't you always make those assumptions on the street—that your opponent has friends, that he's armed and so on? Sometimes bystanders who aren't involved in a fight will start hitting the guy who's winning.

A: I guess they assume the winner is always wrong. Yes, that's a good assumption to make.

Q: Next on the list is the rear-naked choke.
A: Very effective. When I was a bouncer, sometimes I'd just climb on the guy's back, choke him out and take him outside—no harm done. If I had to pick one grappling move to learn, this would be it. But again, don't depend on it against multiple opponents.

Q: How about the triangle choke?
A: In MMA, it's very effective. Guys like Dean Lister are unbelievable with it. For self-defense, it's also great, especially for women. In an attempted rape, the guy has to position himself between the woman's legs, which is exactly where the technique is designed to work. If the attacker doesn't know what a triangle choke is, it's very dangerous. He's saying to himself: "Oh, she's wrapping her legs around my head. So what?" Five seconds later, he's gone.

Q: So a person who doesn't know what a triangle choke is won't see it as a threat.

A: Exactly, and that's what you want. Sometimes people tell women that they should stick a finger in their attacker's eye, but I can tell you, if someone does that to me, more than anything else it makes me angry. I won't let go; I'll pay you back. So I don't know how smart it is to try to poke out the eye of someone who has a dominant position over you. Has he just killed someone? If so, chances are you're going to be killed anyway. So you might as well bite, scream, kick and eye-gouge. But if it's between getting killed and getting raped for a woman, I'd choose getting raped.

With the triangle choke, though, he'll never see it coming. During the setup, he might even start laughing because you're putting your legs around his head. But once it's on, it's over.

Q: What about the cross-body armbar?

A: It's a great technique, but many people in MMA don't do it right. They don't squeeze their knees together. You do that not to control his arm but to keep him from pushing your leg off his head and coming into your guard. That's why I always cross my feet—so he can't push my leg away. Also, with no *gi,* it's hard to control the arm and keep him from rolling out, especially if he's sweaty.

Q: The Americana.

A: It's good because you can rip the guy's arm or shoulder off right away. However, even though it's the most basic arm lock there is, 90 percent of people still do it wrong and the opponent rolls out. The trick is to bring your opponent's hand in the same line as his shoulders, or even lower, and then lift his elbow. Once you do that, he can't roll out because you've locked him up.

The Americana is good for the street, too, because it's a fast move. Once you get it, you jack the shoulder and it's over.

Q: The *kimura*.

A: It depends. On the street, if the guy doesn't know anything, it's a great move. But a woman doing it against a man who's stronger? Probably not so good.

In MMA, though, people know that there are a lot of ways to get out of the kimura. To keep that from happening, you have to do it right. The way I teach it is to put the guy in your guard, then grab the arm and push the back of his hand against his back. It's got to touch his back to make it hard for him to stretch his arm, so bend his arm as much as you can. If you give him two inches of space, he can stretch his arm and escape. Feel free to try this at home to learn the difference it makes.

Q: The *omo plata* and *gogo plata*.

A: Both are a waste of time on the street—unless you're B.J. Penn and you're fighting a single opponent. With normal clothes on, like a pair of jeans, it's very difficult to do either technique. And very few people—Eddie Bravo happens to be one of them—are flexible enough. In MMA, if you're sufficiently limber, be my guest.

Q: The heel hook.

A: It's very effective. I've actually used it on the street against guys who weren't very nice. It works

well because no one knows what it is. One key to making the heel hook work is this: The more his leg is bent, the more effective the technique is. The most effective one is the inverted heel hook, of course.

Q: But if a leg lock fails, doesn't it leave you in a bad position?

A: Not if you give it up and move on. It's like the armbar: If you go for it and your opponent escapes, you can't stay on your back. You have to reposition yourself immediately. Same with leg locks. If you do them the right way, they're good. If you do them the wrong way and lose position, you need to make sure you lock up his hips. But if you place your knees together so he cannot push your legs away and escape, they're very effective. You must train for when a leg lock fails, though. Let your training partner get out of it and learn to reposition yourself—make it a drill.

Q: Then, even if the leg lock doesn't work, you have him locked up and you can transition to something else.

A: Right. Something I recommend—for use by itself or when the heel hook fails—is the inverted heel hook. The normal heel hook is pretty easy to escape from, especially in MMA competition with no shoes and no gi pants. The inverted heel hook, though, is a more solid weapon because the angle is better. It's preferred for the street, too.

But with any technique as effective as the heel hook, you have to think twice before using it for self-defense. I used one against Takahashi Yoshiki in a Pancrase match and broke his shinbone. His shin was apparently weaker than his knee. Is that something you really want to do on the street? Probably not, unless he's a very bad guy.

DIEGO SANCHEZ

Meet The Ultimate Fighter!

*Diego Sanchez, poster boy
of the mixed martial arts.*

by Robert W. Young,
photos by Rick Hustead
Black Belt August 2005

You've got to like a guy who's just proved he's one of the most skilled mixed martial artists in the world, then shyly admits to having Bruce Lee—"He was 50 years ahead of his time"—and Rickson Gracie—"My dream is to roll with him one day if he'll give me the opportunity"—as his role models.

Meet Diego Sanchez, the 23-year-old native of Albuquerque, New Mexico, who commanded four of the most decisive wins seen on Spike TV's *The Ultimate Fighter* reality series. Having been awarded a much-hyped "six-figure contract" with the Ultimate Fighting Championship for his efforts, he's sure to become a familiar face to MMA fans around the world.

Kenpo and Wrestling Roots

Like many *Black Belt* readers, Sanchez got his start in the arts because of the violent environment in which he was raised. "I grew up in a rough neighborhood with a lot of bullies," he says. "It was either fight back against them or get beat up every day."

His parents signed him up for *kenpo* lessons at age 9. He trained for three years and earned his green belt before throwing in the towel. The incident that launched him on the road to MMA stardom was also the straw that broke the camel's back with respect to point karate. "I got screwed at a tournament and cried," he says. "My parents said, 'That's it; we're putting you in wrestling like your cousins.' I was amped to start wrestling because I was very competitive, and I didn't like the point system of karate. When it's in the judges' hands every single time, it's not a real competition."

His enthusiasm would soon hit a snag, however, when the pudgy youth found out he'd be competing against a plethora of conditioned athletes—little though they were. Nevertheless, he managed to win most of the time.

"I kept wrestling and played football in middle school," Sanchez says. "In high school, for the first time in my life, I had to cut weight—which meant I wasn't a chubby kid anymore. I went through a tough season getting beat by the varsity guys. There was loss after loss after loss, maybe 15 in a row. It showed me how much I hated to lose, but it set the tone, and I started driving myself to change that. I became a year-round wrestler. I learned how hard I could push my body without breaking. I was getting stronger and faster. I learned how to excel."

In his junior year, Sanchez ruled Albuquerque. He even made it to the semifinals at the New Mexico State Championships. "After doing that, I thought, I can do anything," he says. "The next year, I dominated the competition. I had offers for college scholarships, but I turned them all down because I didn't want to cut weight anymore. I was 18 and wanted to grow to my full abilities."

The work ethic he learned and the mind-set he acquired lay the foundation for the success he's enjoying in MMA after such a short time. He now sports an 18-0 record—most of his bouts have been in King of the Cage, so the competition has been tough—and he's never been submitted in the ring. "I've done that all in three and a half years," he says. "I view it as a good way to get some experience. I didn't want to jump right in and try to fight the champion. I needed to build myself up. For me, it's all about being well-rounded."

Bigger and Better Things

Sanchez's mission to become well-rounded in MMA took a giant leap forward when he walked into Jackson's Submission Fighting. There, he met Greg Jackson, MMA coach extraordinaire. "I'd been watching the UFC since I was 9—mowing lawns and pulling weeds to get money for the pay-per-view," Sanchez says. "When I walked into Greg's school, I knew about submissions; I just didn't know how to do them. Within two months, I'd won my first tournament."

Sanchez's rapid advances in submission wrestling prompted Jackson to promote him to the intermediate class. "Then I was tapping guys who were advanced, so I went to advanced," he says. "And I kept winning."

In no time, the Sanchez work ethic reared its

head again, this time after a couple of serious injuries. He broke his foot while training but opted to continue his workouts whenever possible. "I also had a torn pectoral tendon, but I trained through it," he says. "For three months, I grappled with one arm, and it improved my game tremendously. Some things are blessings in disguise."

In 2003 he went pro. "I was so hungry and driven," he says. "I would do a fight, then do a grappling tournament, then do another fight. For me, as a martial artist, this was my life, my sport and my art."

His quest to continually improve his skills has led him to sample every facet of fighting, then pick his favorites to focus on. "For the ground, I love submission wrestling," he says. "I love ground and pound. It's an art."

Early on, Sanchez learned the value of the *muay Thai* offense—the hard way. "I walked into my first professional fight, and the guy, a kickboxer, busted me right in the face," he says. "He hit me so hard, I saw stars. I got cut. Then I went to my corner and thought, Is this really what I want to do for a living? But I had too much pride to let him beat me, so I went back in and choked him out. Then I went home and looked in the mirror and thought, I'm going to have to learn some kickboxing."

Now, he's partial to the knee thrust. "My Thai-boxing instructor, Mike Winklejohn—he's a three-time world champion—and I were doing warm-ups on knees. He said, 'Because of your body style, you have a very powerful knee.' I learned the technique two days before a fight with a good wrestler. I thought I would try it, and 15 knees later, he was hurting real bad. It worked, and if it works, keep doing it. Being able to grab someone's head and pull his face or ribs into my knee—it's just so effective."

The rest of muay Thai didn't do as much for Sanchez. Its elbow strikes seemed OK, he says, but he preferred plain old punching. He admits to having taken a liking to leg kicks, but pouring any amount of serious time into kick training all too often resulted in his getting sidelined with an injury.

With a taste of Thai-style hand work under his belt, Sanchez did what any self-respecting experimentalist would do: He scheduled himself for a professional boxing match without ever having fought an amateur bout. "I did it because I wanted to have to concentrate on nothing but boxing," he says. "It was fun. It was a good change. I scored a second-round knockout."

In addition to being fun, the bout of pure pugilism taught the budding MMA fighter a valuable lesson: "I found that there's a big difference between boxing and kickboxing. It's in the setups and the footwork. When kicks and knees aren't allowed, it changes everything."

Strategic and Philosophical Principles

Obviously, versatility is required for success in the MMA ring, Sanchez says. But it's not nearly enough. "Nowadays in the UFC, the guys are all so well-rounded in grappling, striking and kicking that it comes down to conditioning and heart and who wants it more," he says. "It's also about having your mind, body and spirit in line. And you need a good coach, a good manager and training partners. Even then, it doesn't always go your way. Life is what God gives you."

As soon as he sets foot in the octagon, Sanchez's strategy is simple: Be aggressive. "I believe in animal instinct," he says. "I believe I'm an animal when I get in the ring, and I see my opponent as prey. You may be my friend before a fight, but when the door closes and I'm looking you dead in the eyes, I'm going for the kill. I've said it over and over: I'm a pit bull, and I'll take out the neck—just like an animal in the wild."

Because the specifics of his strategy vary according to the strong points of his opponent's game, it seems only natural that the most challenging matches arise when he's facing someone he has no knowledge of. "It makes you cautious," he says. "You have to respect him because you don't know how good he is. Sometimes you win, and sometimes it's a lesson. You might try to take him down and get kneed in the face. So you try something else."

One thing he advises all would-be champs to get to know up close and personal is what it feels like to get hit in the head. "Like in anything, you have to work your way up," he says. "Buy a pair of 16-ounce gloves and some headgear. Find an opponent who's at your level or maybe a little below it—you're not going in there to knock his head off. You'll find that getting hit in the head is the same whether your eyes are open or closed. So keep your eyes open and see that punch coming. Feel it. The next time, it won't be so bad. Then work your way up with someone who's a little tougher and hits a little harder."

Once you've become intimate with pain, it's time to work on your mental attributes, Sanchez says. "Because it's a game of chess in the ring, I'm big on meditation. I visualize my hand getting raised in victory. I visualize the fans. I visualize hugging my mom afterward. I visualize every part of the fight, every technique. It makes your mind that much faster because you've already gone through it. It's like doing your homework in college and then getting a job. You're better prepared than the competition."

Strength and Conditioning Secrets

When it comes to training, Sanchez says he'll try any kind of workout. "And I'll have fun doing it. A while ago, I took up break dancing as a hobby—and for strength conditioning, flexibility and agility. It's fun, and it teaches you how to move and generate power from any position. Dancing is about rhythm, and fighting has a lot to do with rhythm. If you can incorporate that into your mind, you can fight better."

Until a recent injury, he honed his cardio by running hills and mountains near his hometown in the Southwest. Now he relies on other methods—including dancing and yoga, which bolsters conditioning, strength and flexibility. To build his muscles and joints, he concentrates on free-weight exercises. "The joints are the weakest part of the body, and you're only as strong as your weakest part," he says. "To strengthen them, I do rehabilitation-therapy exercises like the ones you do when you're hurt. Then I just increase the weight and reps when I need to."

But when he's ready to get down to business, Sanchez is a firm believer in specificity of training. "To condition myself for a fight, I do grappling and fighting," he says. "I go round after round—what we call the Circle of Death. There are 12 guys, and after every five minutes, you get a fresh guy. You only get a one-minute break."

To survive pseudo-death matches like that, a fighter needs to be able to see an opportunity and seize it, he says. To do that, he has to be fluent in the techniques and have established the

muscle memory that comes from having done them thousands of times. "The opening lasts only a fraction of a second, then it's gone," he says. "You have to go for it."

Go for it is exactly what Sanchez did in every bout he competed in on *The Ultimate Fighter* and in King of the Cage before that. Despite the massacres he inflicted on his opponents, success hasn't swelled his head. "I'm still a student," he says. "I know what I know, but I'm still learning. I don't believe in reaching a peak. I think you can always get better. My goal is to be the most well-rounded fighter in the world. I have the assets. I'm open-minded, and with that mentality, I'm going all the way to the top."

And after that? "When I retire, I want to run a school and teach," he says. "I want to get certified in yoga and teach that, also. But before then— probably within the next year or two—you'll see me in some fight scenes in movies. But I'm not trying to become some big actor; I'm concentrating on fighting because that's what I'm best at."

WELCOME TO MY NIGHTMARE

by Jon Thibault
Black Belt August 2005

Q: In *The Ultimate Fighter,* did you change your game plan depending on whether you faced a wrestler like Josh Koscheck or a *jiu-jitsu* stylist like Kenny Florian?
A: Every fight has a different game plan. With Koscheck, it was a lot different. I'd gone day in and day out for 60 days, teaching him everything I knew to help his game. We would train hard against each other and make each other better. It was awkward. We were best friends and training partners, but then it was like: "OK, it's business. I know I want it more than you do."

Q: It must have been difficult because you'd taught him defenses to many of your moves.
A: Exactly. In the last couple of weeks of training, I realized he was really susceptible to the guillotine, and I hadn't been using it on him. I got him once or twice in practice with it. Then I got him in a guillotine at the very end of the first round [of our fight], and it would have been another five grand for me if I'd had just two more seconds.

Q: Before fighting Florian in the season finale, you thought he would be one of your toughest opponents. During the match, however, he didn't seem to pose much of a challenge. What do you think he did wrong?
A: I don't think it's necessarily what he did wrong; I think it's what I did right. Kenny's an awesome fighter, and a lot of guys on the show even thought that he was going to out-strike me. He prepared for me by working his *muay Thai* and boxing a lot, but he didn't train with a 230-pound guy on top of him the way I did. I have a great team, and I have excellent teammates. I knew he didn't have anybody to really put it to him the way I did.

When I was going into the finals, I knew we were both very good grapplers, but there was a difference: I could take him down, and he couldn't take me down. I knew I was going to be on top, throwing the leather. And that's exactly what happened. I didn't expect it to go so good,

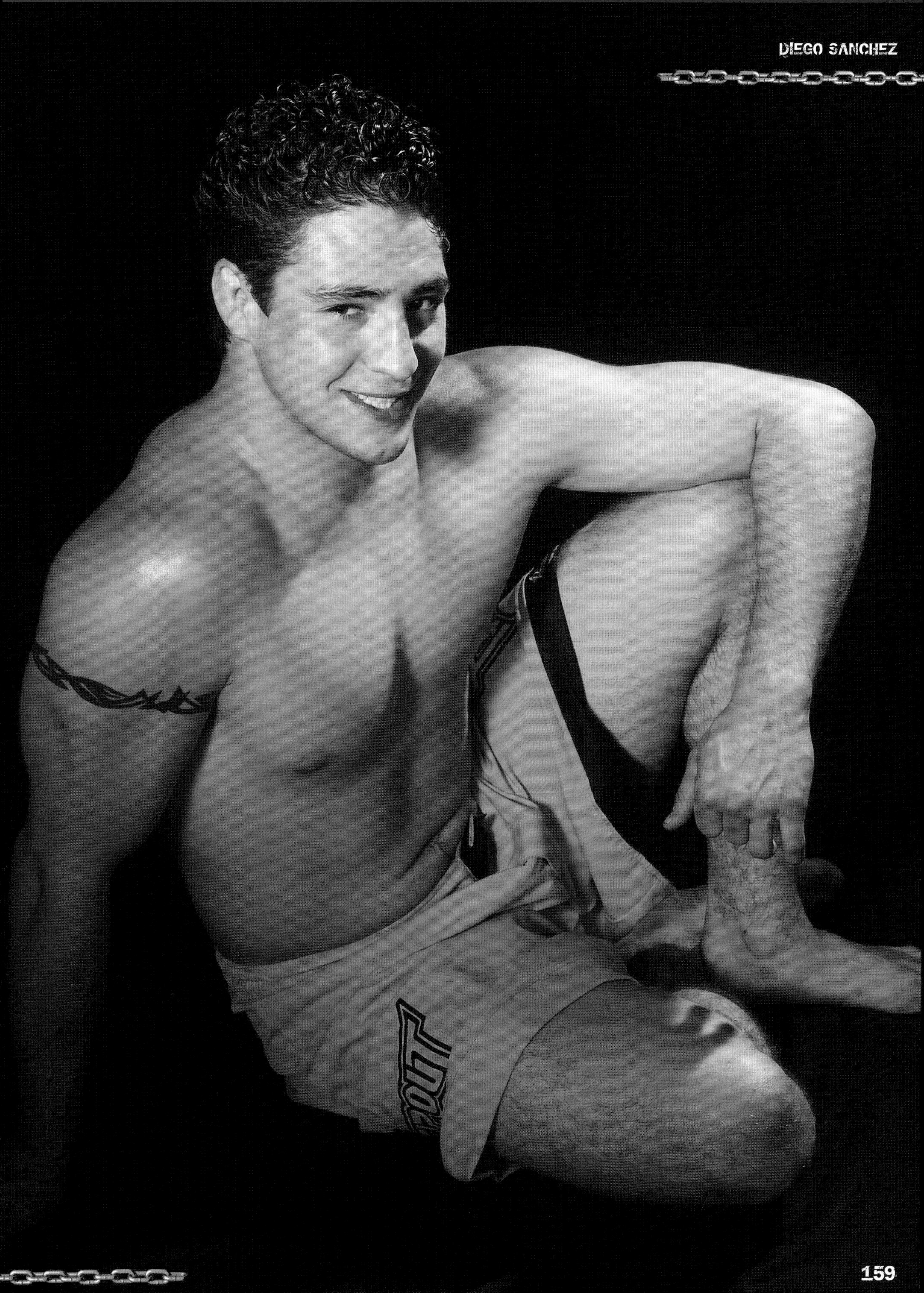

The show and the fights I've had up until now are just a prelude, just a little intro to what's to come in the future. Mark my words: I'm going to be the UFC champ at 170 and at 185. My goal was to win the show, come into the UFC, be the most marketable person the UFC has ever seen, and cater to the Hispanic and Latino fans of boxing who haven't come over to mixed martial arts yet. There are millions of them, and they haven't crossed over yet. My goal is to bring those people to MMA, grow our sport and dominate in the UFC.

FRANK SHAMROCK

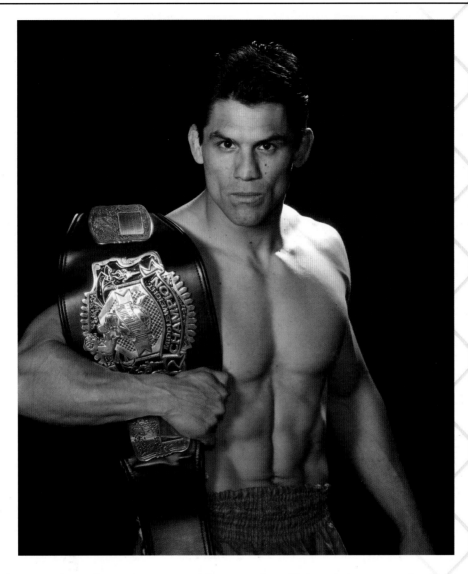

The Other Side of Frank Shamrock

by Edward Pollard, photos by Rick Hustead
Black Belt January 2008

Q: Is there a particular art you'd like to be more familiar with?
A: *Tai chi.* I think it's one of the better healing and focusing arts. I'm into a lot of healing these days.

Q: At what point in your life did you truly feel like a mature adult?

A: I'm hoping that's around 40. I've got about five more years.

Q: Do you have any tattoos?
A: Yes. I have one tattoo. It's a feather on my toe. It's in reference to my Native American heritage. There's a belief that when you're a young man,

if you focus hard enough, you can fly. So I put a feather on my toe to help.

Q: Do you have a hobby that has nothing to do with mixed martial arts?
A: Just reading. And being outside. I like to be outside. I don't want to sleep there, but I like being on the earth and in the sun. It's a good place to be, feet on the ground and looking at the sky.

Q: If you'd taken another direction in life besides fighting and the martial arts, what might that have been?
A: I would've been a physical therapist and a history teacher. I love history. I think it's the future of our people because [otherwise] we're going to do the same thing over and over. If you study history, you'll learn more about who you are and who we are.

Q: What's the most important thing parents can give their children?
A: Parents need to give their kids a sense of self-worth. That's probably the biggest thing that kids don't have.

Q: Is self-worth difficult to pass on?
A: It's difficult because most parents are lacking in it. We see it a lot in the martial arts where the parents really need the lesson but are bringing their children there to learn. They're realizing that they can't teach their kids something they don't have or know.

Q: You're an adventurous guy. Is there any activity or endeavor that you've wanted to do but haven't?
A: I've been sky diving, bungee jumping, sword fighting and everything horribly dangerous you could imagine. I don't really desire it so much anymore. My 19-year-old son almost died last year. He was training to be a sword swallower and hurt himself doing it, so that kind of ended my wild, do-anything streak. The next thing on my list is to shoot guns. It's not really hard, but it just sounds like fun.

Q: You seem to relish being a maverick. Where does that come from?
A: I like to live in the truth and tell the truth. It makes me unpopular with people who want to make lots of money [from] people who don't have the information.

Q: Were you a loner as a teenager?
A: I've always been my own self, doing my own thing. Being in this sport was the first time I realized how important it is to be yourself, be truthful and stand for something. The biggest thing this sport has given me is the realization that you have to be real and you have to be truthful; otherwise, you're not a good martial artist and you're not a good person.

Q: What's your favorite martial arts-themed movie?
A: *Enter the Dragon.* The philosophy, ideas and energy tell a lot about life. It's truth, and that's why it's always going to be there.

Q: What's the strangest business proposition you've received?
A: There are so many weird things, but the strangest one was a guy who wanted to make a perfume out of my sweat.

Q: What's the biggest risk you've taken and won?
A: It would be my return to fighting. It would be all the fighting because I was never a fighter. I never cared about fighting; I was a martial artist.

Q: How's your school doing?
A: Fantastic. We're opening two more schools by the first quarter of next year. We've really branched out with our charity work. I'm working with the autistic community in San Jose. We're in deep, and I feel this school is the heart of the martial arts community here.

Q: Name something that's special about your school.

A: I've got the canvas from my fight with [Phil] Baroni on the wall. I made a ring with six ropes, and instead of traditional ropes, it's like a cargo net. Since it's a ring and a cage, I call it the "rage." I hand-sewed the corner pads with my wife's sewing machine and used some of the canvas from the Baroni fight.

Q: If you were the editor of *Black Belt,* who would you put on the cover?

A: I don't know. Certainly not me. The only person I can think of would be my boxing coach, Tony Demaria. He's a true martial artist and doesn't even know it—like I never knew it. I started fighting with no knowledge of fighting or the martial arts. I became a martial artist because everything you need to be a good martial artist is necessary to survive as a professional fighter. All the things came to me organically. I had to stretch because I was tight. I had to learn massage because I had muscle trauma. I had to learn meditation because I had to deal with these huge, stressful events. Tony is a wonderful martial artist, and he doesn't even know it.

Warrior Yoga

Frank Shamrock harnesses the power of the ancient art for modern no-holds-barred competition.

by Drew Archer and Edward Pollard
Black Belt October 2004

The traditional martial arts have always focused on training the body, mind and spirit, and they've served practitioners well for thousands of years. However, during the past decade, a new method has emerged. It's an innovative approach built on the freedom to learn from all styles without regard for why a particular skill was created or where it originated. It's been dubbed the "mixed martial arts."

Like traditional martial artists, MMA enthusiasts focus on physical training and conditioning. By subjecting their bodies to unfamiliar demands, they transform themselves into some of the most well-rounded athletes in the world. Heavy-duty cardio workouts, weightlifting sessions and sparring matches all play an important role in their daily routines.

Because they constantly test their skills in the ring, they're always in need of more efficient ways to respond to the stresses they face. They already know it pays to study a variety of fighting disciplines and blend the best techniques into a cohesive whole. That has made the technical side of the martial arts grow by leaps and bounds during the past 10 years.

Unfortunately, many of these athletes have been so focused on developing their physique that they've neglected the mental and spiritual aspects of the traditional arts. They're just starting to discover that competition challenges the brain as much as the body. They're learning that having a mechanism to cope with the mental ups and downs of limited-rules combat is vital to success. For a few of them, that mechanism is a modern interpretation of a centuries-old discipline from India: yoga.

Connecting

Frank Shamrock, one of the premier MMA fighters in the world, long ago recognized the value of incorporating yoga into a holistic approach to the mixed martial arts. Renowned for using cross-training to kick, punch and grapple his way to the top of the food chain, he relied on yoga to keep his mind and body in optimal shape. Before a bout, he would use it to prepare mentally and physically, and afterward he would use it to heal any injuries he sustained.

Soon after discovering the value of yoga, Shamrock ran into Jeremy Corbell, creator of an entity known as Warrior Yoga. He immediately knew he'd found someone who could understand what he needed in terms of training, healing and sustaining his energy levels despite constant pressure from within and without. In many ways, the two had been operating on parallel tracks, and each offered the other the experience and wisdom he'd gleaned from his chosen field.

"Warrior Yoga is his program, his philosophy," Shamrock says. "My experience is in training. I did a lot of similar techniques in stretching and working out, so when we started to train together, there was a lot of the same thing going on. He had targeted areas of the body and developed a mentor approach that I'd had for fighting but not for general conditioning or life."

Once he delved into Warrior Yoga, Shamrock noticed he was getting injured less often because his body was more balanced and toned, he says. He also identified two other areas in which big improvements were made: stretching and meditation.

Stretching

Early in his career, Shamrock learned that stretching should be a major component of all serious

training programs, but even as MMA competition rose to prominence, many athletes considered it taboo. Nevertheless, he adjusted his training accordingly, and he still enjoys the benefits of regularly elongating his muscles, which can boost strength and explosive power.

"I use the stretching portion of Warrior Yoga for general conditioning and balance training, as well as for breathing and relaxing," he says. "I like to go through 10 basic postures—most are on the mat but a couple are standing. I like to go through the range of flexion. I think of yoga as a slowed-down version of a mat drill or *kata.*"

The physical side of yoga practice benefits martial arts training because it's conditioning- and balance-oriented, he says. "Striking is very aerobic; you maximize your body in the upright position, which is cardiovascular. Your center of balance and speed give you distance and the ability to do damage. Yoga is nice because it reinforces your balance.

"For grappling, you need conditioning and technique, and yoga goes right to the source of conditioning."

Shamrock likes to complete a yoga workout before and after training, sparring, wrestling and teaching. "I use it to heat up—to stress or warm up certain areas of my body—and reinforce the techniques physically," he says. "I usually take 10 or 15 minutes before any really strenuous workout and do a calming, stretching, energizing yoga workout. When I do it, I keep in mind the technique, concept or theory I'm going to train."

Meditation

Yoga practice is designed to take students to the edge of their physical capacity. They quickly find that holding the poses for any length of time reveals the limitations of their flexibility, thus helping them learn how to recognize pain as a marker and not simply a warning. For fighters, meditation and focused breathing are the keys to tolerating the burning sensation that accompanies the stretch.

Pain management becomes crucial because every serious yoga student courts this edge of performance to measure his progress. Shamrock is keenly aware of what happens at that edge and uses meditation to still his mind when he gets there. "I start with the breath and lengthen it out a bit," he says. "Whatever I'm thinking of, I breathe it away. Whatever is there, I say, 'OK, that's really not necessary,' and exhale it with my breath."

Obviously, deep breathing is an integral part of yoga meditation. In a prolonged battle, remembering to breathe properly can be challenging. Normal or shallow breathing is reflexive, but focused breathing doesn't come naturally. It must be learned.

For Shamrock, a typical meditation/breathing session lasts from five minutes to 10 minutes and involves soft lighting, music and a peaceful environment. During that time, he strives to achieve a higher level of awareness by emptying his mind—by warming up his brain to do nothing, he says. In everyday terms, it involves reducing the amount of attention paid to distracting thoughts, especially those that arise in response to the pain induced by stretching.

When Shamrock is ready to go deep into a meditative state, he often combines a form of self-hypnosis with a long walk, thus lowering his energy output. Gradually he adds layers of intent back into his consciousness until he's ready to begin acting physically again. It's the ultimate preparation for the ultimate sport.

Potential

The Shamrock-Corbell partnership has given rise to a new level of understanding in the mixed martial arts. By sharing information about the worlds of athletic and holistic training, they've resurrected the true design and purpose of fighting arts that were created millennia ago: the melding of the body, mind and spirit. The martial arts community is better off because of it.

GEORGES ST. PIERRE

A Not-So-Private Lesson

What martial artists can learn from the stunning success of UFC champ Georges St. Pierre!

by Robert W. Young, photos by Edward Pollard
Black Belt May 2009

Even if you're not a fan of the Ultimate Fighting Championship, by now you've probably heard about the ease with which Georges St. Pierre systematically dismantled B.J. Penn at the UFC 94. The victory is just part of a five-bout winning streak for the 27-year-old Canadian karateka. If that doesn't sound like much, look back a bit further and you'll see that he's lost only two of his past 12 matches—both of which he later avenged. In case you don't have enough time to dissect all those battles, we thought we'd give you a breakdown of how he does it and how you can apply the lessons the champ has learned the hard way.

—Editor

Observation: "Georges St. Pierre is a gifted athlete," says Lito Angeles, author of *Fight Night! The Thinking Fan's Guide to Mixed Martial Arts.* "He was blessed with exceptional athleticism."

Explanation: That includes balance and an abundance of fast-twitch muscle fibers, Angeles says. "You see his superior balance in the way he's able to thwart takedowns. In his fight with Josh Koscheck, Koscheck tried to take him down. GSP did a catlike movement and managed to land on his feet. It was spectacular. No matter who he's fighting, he's always in a good position to do what he wants, whether he's standing, in a clinch, doing a takedown, neutralizing a takedown or getting to side control. "Fast-twitch muscle fibers give him the capacity for explosive movements."

Action: "For the most part, you're born with a certain amount of fast-twitch muscle fibers, but you can enhance what you have to some degree," Angeles says. "It's the same for balance: You're born with it, but it can be honed through hard training in the various disciplines that cover stand-up fighting, the clinch and the ground."

Observation: "GSP has a work ethic that's second to none," Angeles says. "He trains hard in a number of fighting disciplines with world-class people, and he doesn't mind if he gets his butt kicked. Then he takes techniques from those disciplines and fits them into the MMA framework."

Explanation: Everybody he trains with is better than he is at that particular art, Angeles says. "For example, he works out with Otis Grant, who's a former world boxing champion. If GSP fought Grant in a boxing match, he'd probably lose, but if he fought Grant or any of his other training partners in MMA, GSP would win because he combines the skills better."

Action: Don't limit your training partners to just people you can beat. Spar with students who have a good chance of beating you, and when they do, learn from them. It's the only way to get better.

Observation: GSP has deadly hands.
Explanation: "He trains in boxing, but he doesn't use conventional boxing in the octagon," Angeles says. "He modifies it so his stance is a little wider, which enables him to counter takedowns better. And his distancing is a little farther away, which means his opponent doesn't know if he's going to punch or kick."

Action: If you're into MMA, study conventional boxing but don't plan on using it as is in competition because you'll be taken down, Angeles says. "The best place to learn MMA-modified boxing is in an MMA gym. It's not a bad thing to study conventional boxing because it will teach you the body mechanics needed to throw hard punches," he says.

"If you're more into self-defense than MMA and you had to pick one established system to learn, it should be boxing," Angeles says. I'd modify it to use the palms instead of the fists because the palms have more structural integrity. Anything you can do with your fists, you can do with your palms."

Observation: GSP can kick like a mule.
Explanation: "He has great kicking skills because of his karate background," Angeles says. "His lead-leg round kick shows a *kyokushin* and *muay Thai* influence, but it's not pure kyokushin or pure muay Thai. He makes his kicks fast and snappy. He doesn't try to put full power into each one and blast his opponent to death. He uses mostly round kicks, delivered from either leg. His lead-leg kicks are very effective even though they were considered worthless in the early days of MMA. In his second fight with Matt Hughes, he knocked him down with a lead-leg kick.

Action: Study a hard-core kicking art like kyokushin or muay Thai, but remember that the techniques may not work unless you adapt them to MMA. "You have to be able to seamlessly integrate the kicks with punches, takedowns and takedown defense," Angeles says.

Observation: GSP knows knees and elbows.
Explanation: "He uses them mostly on the ground, where he blends them with punches,"

Angeles says. "You don't really see him use elbows while he's standing or in the clinch. He's a good clinch fighter, but he's more likely to peck at you with strikes or just take you down."

Action: Even though GSP is sufficiently skilled to avoid having to fight in the clinch, you may not be so fortunate. Work on your clinch-fighting skills in case you're trapped in that position, Angeles says. Muay Thai is a great place to start.

Observation: GSP recognizes the value of Brazilian *jiu-jitsu.*

Explanation: "He trains with a world-class team in Canada and periodically goes to Brazil to work out," Angeles says. "When he's on the ground, he doesn't mind being in his opponent's guard—he'll just pound him. That's when he uses the elbows."

Action: Learn jiu-jitsu now, and if you want to compete in MMA, train without a *gi.*

Observation: GSP has equipped himself with the submissions, escapes and reversals he needs to fight and win on the ground.

Explanation: "However, he hasn't really had to use them," Angeles says. "So far, he's always been dominant on the ground. He's the one who's usually on top. But he did use an armbar to submit Hughes in their third fight."

Action: When it comes to grappling techniques, Angeles says, you should focus on the basics—the armbar, *kimura,* rear-naked choke and triangle. "Forget about having a trick that no one else has seen. All the holds that are effective are being used. Why do fighters get caught in them? Because they work. There are more tricks when a gi is worn because you have more handles, but MMA is different."

Observation: GSP is a fantastic wrestler—in fact, he trains with the Canadian Olympic Team.

Explanation: "You see both Greco-Roman and freestyle wrestling—Greco-Roman in the clinching and freestyle in the takedowns," Angeles says.

"He's the best takedown artist in MMA right now."

Action: "Pick a base art according to what you gravitate to, but know that wrestling is generally regarded as the best base because of its training methodologies," Angeles says. "In addition to developing great balance and teaching you how to execute and counter takedowns, wrestling is easily mixed with techniques from other arts. Most MMA fighters who come from wrestling are able to pick up the necessary striking skills easily.

"Unfortunately, there are few wrestling schools for adults. Your best option is to go to a local high school, junior college or university and speak with the wrestling coach. He may not let you practice, but you might be able to hook up with someone with the same interests."

Observation: GSP is a master of the mental game.
Explanation: "He's proved that he's mentally strong," Angeles says. "Even though he lost to Matt Serra and Matt Hughes, he had a winning streak before and after and avenged both losses. Either loss could have broken a lesser fighter, but GSP used them to improve himself."

Action: Part of mental strength comes from the environment you were raised in, Angeles says. "But it definitely can be developed—to a greater extent than physical attributes, even. The best way to do that is through rigorous physical preparation. When I interviewed Georges, I asked him how he strengthens himself before a fight. He said, 'It's all in the preparation.' It's like studying hard before a test."

Observation: GSP uses visualization to program himself for success.
Explanation: "He pumps himself up with positive thoughts, seeing himself winning and putting himself in difficult situations and getting out of them," Angeles says.

IT RUNS IN THE FAMILY

by Stephen Quadros
Black Belt May 2009

When your father is a black belt, like Georges St. Pierre's is, and you've practiced the martial arts since you were 7, it instills a pure-hearted conviction and confidence that transcend the limits of the jock/animal syndrome that's so much the vogue at the lower levels of the combat sports today. In this rare case, a world-class athlete like St. Pierre has been born into a special situation, with an upbringing in a traditional martial arts household, that set a foundation for him to achieve his dreams. And the Ultimate Fighting Championship welterweight has done just that.

Having a paternal hero will always leave an impression that a child will follow for a lifetime. As St. Pierre himself said: "Growing up, of course, as every other kid, I thought my dad was the toughest guy in the world. He was a black belt, and I remember when he broke a brick in front of me and my friends. And we were like, 'Whoa!' " I am sure that the children of the late Helio Gracie—Rickson, Royce, Royler, Rorion, et al—were given the natural gift of a similar mind-set from their father. It all but guarantees great things.

So far, the mixed martial arts have seen the powerful influences of *jiu-jitsu*, wrestling, boxing and *muay Thai,* but for the most part, the traditional arts have been ignored and at times maligned. Until now. I'm not one who believes that a style can make you a better fighter, give you values or make you more disciplined. Those kinds of metamorphic changes happen when you have a calm mental attitude, a trusting relationship with your teacher and the readiness to accept growth without any negative side effects or distractions, like ego and self-destructive behavior. So the combination of being born a super-athlete and raised in a martial environment that's steeped in tradition has created an unstoppable force. Samurai spirit at the top of MMA? You bet!

SHAMROCK ON ST. PIERRE

by Edward Pollard
Black Belt March 2009

Q: What makes Georges St. Pierre a champion?
A: He's always learning and developing his techniques specifically for his next opponent. He develops his body along with his mind. His techniques become more and more refined for his style. He doesn't have a pure boxing or wrestling stance; he has a good mix of all the styles.

Q: Do you think GSP's *kyokushin* karate base is best for the mixed martial arts?
A: They all are. That's the beauty of it, especially with a striking art. It's the balance, the coordination, the timing and the [process of] learning about your body.

Q: What are his strengths with respect to striking?
A: He doesn't have a traditional boxing punch. His hands are fluid, straight and damaging. His punches come from a centering stance that's different from boxing and *muay Thai*. Coming from karate, he stays back a little bit and turns a little more sideways, presenting himself as skinny.

Q: What other factors make him stand out?
A: You have to work your butt off to be a champion, and you have to work twice as hard to stay there—which is where most people fall down. Georges has kept the focus, and he's kept his humility in check.

Q: How does a fighter maintain his conditioning and confidence over time?
A: It's all about the people you surround yourself with. They help you stay focused for the long term.

Action: You can create the same kinds of virtual fights and envision yourself overcoming the odds. "Just accept that you're a human being who can be caught at any time," Angeles says. "If that happens, don't let it set you back."

Observation: GSP strategizes.
Explanation: He studies his opponents, Angeles says. "He tries to figure out his opponent's strengths and use them against him. Against Koscheck, GSP out-wrestled him. Beating a guy at his best thing can get into his brain."
Action: If you compete at a level that allows you to know who your next opponent will be, study the way he fights, Angeles says. Against an unknown adversary on the street, think pre-emption. "You have to read the pre-fight indicators and attack first," Angeles says. "You should always assume that he's as good or better than you, that he's carrying a weapon and that he has friends. Strike first. This is how a lesser-skilled person can beat a more-skilled person. It's where MMA and self-defense part ways. Sport fighting is technically more difficult than street fighting, but street fighting has greater potential consequences."

BIBLIOGRAPHY

Alonso, Marcelo. "The Phenom Is Back: The Life and Times of Brazil's Most Popular MMA Fighter: Vitor Belfort." *FightSport* October/November 2003: 36-39.

Angeles, Lito. "The Pride of PRIDE: The Techniques, Tactics and Training of Welterweight Champion Dan Henderson." *Black Belt* August 2006: 74-80.

---. "Technique Critique: Fighting Legend Bas Rutten Rates the Best and the Worst Moves in the Martial Arts! Part One." *Black Belt* August 2007: 78-86.

---. "Technique Critique: Fighting Legend Bas Rutten Rates the Best and the Worst Moves in the Martial Arts! Part Two." *Black Belt* September 2007: 112-119.

---. "Technique Critique: Fighting Legend Bas Rutten Rates the Best and the Worst Moves in the Martial Arts! Part Three." *Black Belt* October 2007: 112-118.

Angeles, Lito and **Edward Pollard**. "Quinton Jackson vs. Forest Griffin." *Black Belt* May 2008: 84-89.

Archer, Drew and **Edward Pollard**. "Warrior Yoga: Frank Shamrock Harnesses the Power of the Ancient Art for Modern No-Holds-Barred Competition." *Black Belt* October 2004: 135-139.

Callos, Tom. "Full-Contact Fighter of the Year: Gina Carano." *Black Belt* December 2007: 130.

Cheng, Dr. Mark. "The Chinese Connection." *Black Belt* December 2008: 87.

Editors of Black Belt. "Up Close and Personal With Kyra Gracie: Meet the Newest Star of the Legendary Brazilian Grappling Family!" *Black Belt* June 2008: 106-111.

Ford, Willard. "But Seriously, Folks…" *FightSport* Winter 2002: 32-35.

George, Christian. "MMA Exclusive: Matt Hughes on Training, Fighting and Winning." *Black Belt* February 2008: 122-127.

---. "A Man of Faith." *Black Belt* February 2008: 125.

Gross, Josh. "Head Games." *FightSport* Fall 2002: 30-32.

---. "Randy Couture." *FightSport* December 2003/January 2004: 56-60.

McNeil, Jason William. "Fallen Angel." *21st Century Warriors: Fighting Secrets of Mixed-Martial Arts Champions*. 2009: 88.

---. "Gene LeBell: The Godfather of Grappling." *21st Century Warriors: Fighting Secrets of Mixed-Martial Arts Champions*. 2009: 94-101.

---. "Gracie Legacy." *21st Century Warriors: Fighting Secrets of Mixed-Martial Arts Champions*. 2009: 34-38.

---. "Profile: Gokor Chivichyan." *21st Century Warriors: Fighting Secrets of Mixed-Martial Arts Champions*. 2009: 21-27.

---. "Profile: Renato Magno." *21st Century Warriors: Fighting Secrets of Mixed-Martial Arts Champions*. 2009: 122-127.

---. "Profile: Renzo Gracie." *21st Century Warriors: Fighting Secrets of Mixed-Martial Arts Champions*. 2009: 52-56.

---. "Sanshou." *21st Century Warriors: Fighting Secrets of Mixed-Martial Arts Champions*. 2009: 93.

Neklia, Steve. "Helio Gracie: 1997 Man of the Year." *Black Belt* 1997 Yearbook.

Plott, J. Michael. "The Right Stuff." *Black Belt* March 2005: 70.

Pollard, Edward. "Bas Rutten Documentary." *Black Belt* May 2008: 32-34.

---. "B.J. Penn: The Ultimate Fighter's Newest Coach Reveals His Training and Fighting Secrets!" *Black Belt* June 2007: 78-87.

---. "Dan Henderson: 2007 MMA Fighter of the Year." *Black Belt* December 2007: 129.

---. "Gracie Update: Latest News From the Birthplace of Brazilian Jiu-Jitsu in America." *Black Belt* December 2006: 74-82, 138.

---. "Growing up Gracie." *Black Belt* March 2008: 52-54.

---. "Let a New Adventure Begin." *Black Belt* May 2009: 46.

---. "Liddell's Leadership Lesson." *Black Belt* March 2005: 70-73.

---. "Machado Jiu-Jitsu Comes to Comic Books." *Black Belt* September 2008: 36.

---. "The Other Side of Frank Shamrock." *Black Belt* January 2008: 52-54.

---. "Shamrock on St. Pierre." *Black Belt* May 2009: 72.

---. "Tradition Rules! UFC Star Lyoto Machida Makes Old-School Karate Work in MMA." *Black Belt* February 2009: 76-83.

---. "Train to be a Mixed-Martial Arts Champion! Exclusive Interview With Strikeforce Middleweight Titleholder Cung Le." *Black Belt* December 2008: 84-90.

Quadros, Stephen. "It Runs in the Family." *Black Belt* May 2009: 77.

Seong, S.D. "On Winning: The Youthful Wisdom of Mixed-Martial Arts Champ Karo Parisyan." *Black Belt* March 2008: 106-114.

Thibault, Jon. "Q & A: Forrest Griffin." *Black Belt Buyer's Guide* 2007: 105.

---. "Welcome to My Nightmare." Black Belt August 2005: 71.

Young, Robert W. "3 Facets of Grappling: John Machado Explains Why You Need to Know Them All." *Black Belt* June 2007: 130-138.

---. "Meet the Ultimate Fighter! Diego Sanchez, Poster Boy of the Mixed Martial Arts." *Black Belt* August 2005: 66-73.

---. "The Man Who Changed the World: 15 Years After the UFC Was Conceived, Royce Gracie. Looks Back at How His Fighting Art Rocked the Martial Arts!" *Black Belt* January 2008: 84-91.

---. "A Not-So-Private Lesson: What Martial Artists Can Learn From the Stunning Success of UFC Champ Georges St. Pierre!" *Black Belt* May 2009: 72-77.

---. "Worst Case Jiu-Jitsu: 6 Secret Ways to Turn the Tables on an Opponent Who is About to Submit You!" *Black Belt* November 2008: 85-91.

LIST OF CONTRIBUTORS

Marcelo Alonso has been working as a martial arts photojournalist in Brazil since 1992 and has one of the biggest MMA image archives in the sport. In addition to being editor of *Tatame*, one of Brazil's most respected magazines, Alonso is a correspondent for the world's biggest MMA publications.

Lito Angeles is an avid martial arts researcher, writer, practitioner and instructor who began training more than 30 years ago. He is also a Southern California police officer and frequent contributor to *Black Belt*. He is the author of *Fight Night! The Thinking Fan's Guide to Mixed Martial Arts*.

Drew Archer is a freelance writer who contributes to *Black Belt*.

Tom Callos is a freelance writer who frequently contributes to *Black Belt*.

Dr. Mark Cheng is a traditional Chinese-medicine physician, martial arts researcher, author and licensed acupuncturist based in Los Angeles. He is also a contributing editor for *Black Belt* and a certified kettlebell instructor.

Willard Ford was a contributor for *FightSport*.

Christian George is a freelance writer and martial artist.

Josh Gross grew up in 1980s Los Angeles and knew he wanted to work in sports. When he realized that he couldn't be the next Kirk Gibson or Michael Cooper, Gross set his sights on making an impact in sports journalism.

Jason William McNeil is a writer and martial artist whose work regularly appears in *Black Belt*. He is an active student of the martial arts and holds multiple black belts and instructor-level rankings. He wrote original content for this book.

Steve Neklia was a columnist for *Karate/Kung Fu Illustrated* and contributed several articles to *Black Belt*.

J. Michael Plott is a freelance writer who contributes to *Black Belt*.

Edward Pollard is *Black Belt's* managing editor. He's been with *Black Belt* since early 2002.

Stephen Quadros is a contributor to *Black Belt*. He's been a martial arts practitioner, teacher and trainer for more than 15 years, specializing in kickboxing and mixed martial arts. He works as a commentator for Showtime's EliteXC events and England's top MMA show, Cage Rage.

S.D. Seong is a freelance writer and martial artist based in Southern California.

Jon Thibault was the editor of Black Belt Books from 2005 to 2007.

Robert W. Young has been involved with the martial arts for more than 25 years. As *Black Belt's* executive editor, he oversees the editorial content and artistic vision for the magazine, its specialty titles and related books and DVDs.

Check out

blackbeltmag.com/videos

to see behind-the-scenes footage of our most popular authors, martial artists and MMA fighters!

Interviewed by Edward Pollard